Poet's Island

Robert L. Martin

Cyberwit.net
HIG 45 Kaushambi Kunj, Kalindipuram
Allahabad - 211011 (U.P.) India
http://www.cyberwit.net
Tel: +(91) 9415091004
E-mail: info@cyberwit.net

Printed at Repro India Limited.

PREFACE

This is my seventh book with Cyberwit.net. My first six, ***Wings of Inspiration, Rhymes of the Joke Machine, The Air Almighty, Martin's World, Secrets of the Wind, & Mother of Life,*** all available on Amazon and Barnes and Noble online, have all been very well received and available for sale in many different countries around the world.

Something very special happened to me a short while age. I looked into the internet and googled: Poetry of Robert L. Martin. There I discovered that some of my poems have been acknowledged and narrated by some distinguished people. Some were narrated and set to music and video. They must have been reading some of my books. They all did a splendid job, and it was quite an honor. I also discovered that some of my books have been appearing in various advertisements. On the internet, you can also find the various places in the world where my books are being sold. My publisher is doing quite a wonderful job publicizing them.

It took a little more time to write this book (***Poet's Island***) than it took for the preceding ones, and it is a little lengthier. I took the time to keep editing it, so it is the best I could do. I amazed myself at some of the revelations I came up with. There are always new ideas to keep adding to it, but the end has to be "THE" end, and any new revelations will have to wait for my next book. There is no end to creating art, just a segue to the next project.

The content to ***Poet's Island*** is an accumulation of poems that I wrote, mostly about music, poetry, nature, love, philosophy, and a bit of comedy. I never studied poetry and philosophy in school, so I would be deeply embarrassed if anyone asked me about those subjects. All I know about them is what I learned from God, Kahlil Gibran's book

"The Prophet" after reading, digesting it, and drilling it into my head for many years, and also what I learned from Pablo Neruda's books. I am a pianist, so I know something about music. I am a nature lover, and I have loved many women and seen many come and go and thought about why they did, and how I felt when they stayed or left. So I am qualified to write about love and nature. I have a deep love for words and their meanings and how they resonate in my heart and mind. I love to dig them up through my deep thought and meditations.

The first part of ***Poet's Island*** is mostly about how I feel, what makes me tick, and what makes me different from most people. I'm not driven by popular opinion; just my own. I am my own master. A poet has to have a firm grip on a philosophy that he abides by. In order to write to his liking, he has to love and choose the right words. These words have to have an effect upon his heart and come from his heart. If they don't, the God in him that represents love doesn't have anything to do with his writing; therefor it would be a false Messiah that gave him the words and inspiration. I listen to every word that is given to me through the music I listen to and God who is my sole inspirator. I love this book. It comes directly from my heart.

Acknowledgements

This is my seventh book with Cyberwit.net. Thanks to my publisher all my books have been quite successful. The books have reached many countries around the world and received very good reviews. I also have a poetry blog, (Poeticous.com), and have made many friends through it that give me encouragement to keep up the good writing. J Ann Crowder, Grace Chacon Leon, and Nelson Reyes are great writers themselves who are also in the blog.

My daughter Renata again designed the beautiful cover that stands out among the other ones at Barnes and Noble, and my lady friend Linda did some illustrating. I am lucky to be surrounded by so many talented people.

I recited my funny story, *Upon Offending Zombies,* at an open mike session the other night and the audience was howling with laughter. You will find it on page 205 in the book. I love writing comedy too. It makes me happy when I am writing it.

Below are listed all the publishers that gave me permission to use my poems that they published before:

My poems *Chameleon Forest, Upward Pilgrimage, Song of the Pipes, & The Games of Autumn* were previously published by "The Belt and Beyond."

My poems *The Winds of Ambrosia & Inferno Forest* were previously published by "Wilderness House Literary Journal."

My poem *Religionless* was previously published by "Egophobia.ro."

Contents

Sea of Dreams

Sea of dreams of liquid glass,
infusing the real with the unreal,
the quixotic with the mundane,
a journey into the imaginary,

 waters adorned in an aquatic blue,
stretched across the horizon,
flowing across the glassy surface
on the playground of the sea giants
with swirling tails that kick up the waves
and the gentle air that subdues them,
and aquatic angels with celestial fins
who anoint and soothe the waters with their
imperial scepters and infuse
their holy waters into earthen waters,
carve out a pathway to Poet's Island.

"Come ride on boats with hypnotic eyes
that can put you in a trance,
that can bring the unreal before you and
 cast you adrift but in sagacious waters
with assuring sails that know the way,
that have the key to the other world
where imagination can change the ships
into celestrial carriages that can
fly across the universe with one wave
of the magic wand, or can dislodge
Poet's Island from its mooring and
bring it to you.

You are a seafaring passenger
signed up for the ride,
to embark upon a journey
into the imaginary world of the poet."

Poet's Island

Away from the drama and the prosaic
on a shifting isle living in a dream state
where truth is entrenched but forever afloat
on helium soil and purple colored smoke.

Poets settle in but ride the whimsical wind
off to paradise where dreams begin,
flying solo in the warmth of summer's air
on yellow carpets with enhancing flair.

Smiling, gliding, floating on big fat clouds
above the chimneys and the clamoring crowds,
they look at the world through rose colored eyes,
painting over the darkness of the country-sides.

They stroke the paint brushes with love and passion
 and create a new world in a lyrical fashion
while living away from the real-life world
where data is longing to be unfurled,
to loosen up its garments that take away its breath
and sail to Poet's Island with nothing left
and smell the new air that the poets breathe
and think of new stories as they begin to weave.

Away from their homes where data is in control,
 poetry is an alien to keep away from the soul
and poets are the advocates of disorder and chaos
in their stubborn reluctance to get the point across.

But Poet's Island is there to bring joy and elation
and bring to the empty soul a new sensation
while advocating for the two worlds to meet
and form an alliance of admiration complete.

Solitary Man

Solitary man living on his private island,
setting up his own way of life,
faithful to his convictions,
alone in his thoughts and revelations,
miles out at sea but yet upon the shore,
then past the shore into the hinterland
and into the dramas and delights of humanity
with his eyes fastened to their desires and deeds,

collecting words and words beyond,
words that would die if left alone,
words with palpitating desires to
propagate with other words
 and melt into their loving arms
and form a sacred union blessed by the Almighty,

and words with spears that penetrate the heart,
that slither through the fissures of the skin
and reach deep into the jungles of the soul,
words with heated pistons that
drive the engines that drive the thoughts
into primal spaces and spaces beyond,

and words that dig up words buried
deep in the catacombs,
that bring them back to life and
nourish them with the blessed nectar,
putting them into rhythmic stories
and giving them wings to fly with them,

and words that go inside and
mingle with the drama,
that grow fangs that bite into the flesh,
that tear down the walls that joy erected
and pour the sadness into the empty spaces,
bringing the story to you
and letting it settle down in the spirit,

and words that bring joy upon a golden platter,
that paint the sky a bright pastel color,
that lift you up and give you wings,
and invite you to romp with them in the clouds.

 Solitary man, living on his private island,
the little man with big words stuffed inside him,
the unassuming man behind those words,
the instigator of what they do to the spirit,
responsible for the actions of mankind,
is the poet who lives on Poet's Island.

Words and Beyond

Words and beyond and miles of fervor,
roads adorned with golden paint,
 that encircle you and sing to you,
that have arms that reach out and
take you with them to their prophetic paradise,
to their home of warmth and compassion,
knowledge and lore, fantasy and the surreal,

into a story where you can feel its breath,
the story moving inside you
and directing your course,
dancing on your heart
and elevating your spirits,

taking you down the road on
a fiery steed with lofted hooves,
over rose gardens with whetted thorns
and angry rivers and lions' dens,

words with other words attached to them,
that don't strangle them but suggest some more,
that propel the mind and place it
into imaginary settings,
that sit you down upon them
so you can feel them
brushing against your cheek,
their texture, their color, their warmth,
their spirit, their subdued meaning,
their love affair with the sequential word,

the rhetoric that pushes you onto the next,
that instills in your heart a zest to go on and on
and beyond that one lonely word.

Words are not only words but a piston that
drives you on to the next word.

Words Abounding

Swirling above the clouds on high
and below the heavens in the azure sky

ribbons of the rainbow flapping in the wind
forming words where words begin

primal sound tucked in the bosom of silence
waiting to escape through the suffocating fence

to swirl about and dance with the ambrosial rain
and take command from the highest sovereign brain

abounding and multifarious as they form and drift
circling the skies as they ride the clouds and shift

 a new language springing from cerebral tongues
soothing words from the harpist as she strums

words riding on the backs of lightning bolts
screaming in agony as the body jolts

floating into my sphere of understanding and thought
all what heaven and nature hath brought

abounding words to choose from and digest
words of the silence and words of the tempest

words tailored for me to usher into my heart
to soothe my anxieties with a poetic spark

to write a masterpiece above my primal standing
exalted from the prosaic up to Celestial's Landing

oh beautiful words I love to hear and feel
to lock up inside with an everlasting seal

to come out from my earnest supplication
and begin to fuel my emancipation.

Oh love of words I can feel thy breath upon me.
Please stay in my cerebral home and set me free.

Stravinsky the Poet in Me

My poem is not my poem. It belongs to Igor Stravinsky from his
ballet "The Rite of Spring" that moved inside my being and wrote
the words:

"Adoration of the Earth," the first part
took me into another world from the start,

lifting me up with my feet still on the ground,
bringing me up into an exotic ethereal sound,

telling me to forget myself left behind
as magicians do to bamboozle my mind,

pulling my strings as do master puppeteers,
touching my heart and invoking my tears,

 dissonant, soulful sounds stirring up my soul,
ripping up my inhibitions as I lose control,

moving me from the real through time and space,
uprooted me from my world without a trace,

stole my identity and left me with no name
and deemed me a poet of which I became,

a writer with nothing from me but all of him,
all the "Rite of Spring" in my blood and skin,

my fingers that moved the pen in haste
but he who transformed my appetite and taste

from the prosaic to a sphere where I upward climbed
to the world of dreams and proficiency combined,

pouring his thoughts into my empty mind
making me a genius of the poetic kind,

from he who moves my fingers that write my poem,
and the me who marvels at how I've grown,

as I became a puppet on his melodious string,
the me that emerged from his "Right of Spring."

Le Sacre du Printemps

Haunting theme you come alive.
My sleeping passion you so revive.
Primal screams come from the east.
Searing breath I fear the beast.

But as the music floats I come to rest.
I let its fingers touch my flesh.
Like lullabies from weeping angels
heaven's dressed in beads and bangles.

 Beauty is in the eyes of harmony.
Music why thou art so lonely?
You search the skies to bring it home,
summon the Gods to see it roam.

Igor Stravinsky, your song's divine.
It stirs the blood, feels so sublime.
Heaven's crying in open spaces.
Bring it to me in earthly places.

Before we reach the final ending,
softer than the snow's descending,
the end is here so let it scream,
but do not wake me from my dream.
Rites of Spring do not forsake me.

The Home of Rhyme

Where troubadours assemble in the enchanted heart,
softening up the words as the casings depart,
the home of rhyme starts to take form
where poetry and the love of poetry were born.

Aesthetic feelings blossom in this palpitating home
and spirits awaken from their catacombs and roam;
free to jump into this new world of rhyme
and make up words as they start to climb,

Climbing upward and sailing into a spatial silence
to taste the fragrant air and permeating incense,
they are cleansed in the rivers of Elysium
and anointed by the words of a paean.

This new place in the heart so uplifting
where words fly and troubadours sing,
is my sanctuary where I meditate and write
as my spirit comes to life and turns on the light.

Birth of the Poet

As a straight line appeared before his eyes,
it just laid still and rested on the parchment
waiting for him to plunge into the depth of it
and see it as he wanted it to be.

It started to breathe and bend and take shape
and formed into a colossal flying lizard
that spread its wings and lifted him up.

He felt an exhilarating breeze as it filled his lungs
and his heart beat to the pulse of the sacred drums.
He nestled inside the wings that were soft as silk
and were as fragrant to him as his mother's milk.

He saw the graceful pinions churning inside
that functioned to give him a glorious ride;
Then sailed higher than the highest mount,
through more clouds than he could ever count.

He could see the Universe vibrating before him
and the stars going into a melodic spin.
He could hear silent drums giving them support
and feel the pulse inside his resonant door.

He could feel angelic tears filling his heart
and giving him fuel for his eager start,
the poetic man filled with universal lore
from his inaugural journey to heaven's floor.

Then back to earth but not back to earth;
yet his mind still suspended for his new birth.
His feet on the ground in his old, old world
 as his heart broke loose and inhibitions unfurled.

Poet from your recent birth, write me a verse
and spice it up with thy heavenly words.

Life of the Poet

This poet lives in the world but is not part of it,
aware of the trauma but not caught up in it,
free to choose his own world and define it,
free to choose how deep
to plunge into his observations,
able to find an emotion that he feels deeply about,
and find out if it can help him write,
 find out how sensitive he could make himself,
free to let his sensitivity control his thoughts,
free to find the words to describe them,
able to let them instill a certain feeling in him,
to let those feelings dictate how he writes
and write down these private thoughts
and show the world what he thinks in his own way
and beautify them with his well chosen words.

Free to alienate himself from industrial demands
and from the masses who glorify rhetoric
and popularity with its pockets full of money
to offer him for his works that satisfy all their needs
except for him who would debase himself by accepting it,

but dedicated to keep the faith in himself,
to believe his writings have the credibility
to be admired by his readers and most of all, himself.

From his well-chosen words
he elevates his esteem and hopes that
their esteem will be elevated also.

He lives in poverty, not caring about monetary gains.
He lives in his own world away from the crowd.
He is a loner with his own private thoughts.
His intimate partner is his writing and
 God who gave him the resources
to think and find his way into
and through his writing,

that poor lonely man
who lives and dies
only to write down
 his own words.

Death of the Poet

From dust to dust and poets to their crypts
and words go down with sunken ships.
Vibrating words no longer rattle the spine
and the prose no longer tastes that of wine.

The tides and the moon are no longer lovers
and the sea empties out as the twilight hovers.
Romance is a word that lies still in the mind
and the motion of the waves has no rhyme.

Passion is a river with no where to go
and fly with the rivers of the skyward flow
and the voices of the wind and its eternal echoes
  burn up in the heat of the flaming snows.

The real has a hold on the mobile truth
that flies to one another, then gets up to move.
It joined the world of the black and white
and the stillness of the never ending night.

The poets that ride upon the metal clouds
fall back to earth into the common crowds
with their words still left behind and forgotten
as they crash and burn, never to rise up again.

From dust to dust, from the real to the imaginary,
from the poetic to the unreal, then to the real again.

Poetic Stories

To the point but not so to the point,
wandering through the transcendental air,
flying through time clouds with its melodic wings,
wrapping its arms around the stars,
melting the words down to a fervent sigh
with a story that runs around the mind,
along the spine, through the fissures of the heart,
then to the perplexity of the mind,
leaving the curious reader in limbo,

but a story of the truth of the heart's sensation,
the power of words in their poetic order,
the plot distorted and romanticized,
the story dressed up in its finest attire,
abstract thought leading to more abstract thought,
imagination churning like the winds of time,
words growing wings and soaring into the air,
plots becoming irrelevant and forgotten,
truth losing its footing and living upon the sand,
the house of the poet falling into the sea,

his heart left open for all to peak into,
to see the engines that run his thoughts,
his theories that he lives by,
his mind stuffed full of words and stories,
still unrefined, unfinished, unsettled,
but there to be elaborated upon,
there to add onto each other and
go on and on and on————

Nights of the Day

Nighty dreams amid the hours of the day,
stories controlled by cerebral reins,
not sent adrift on the high seas
as dreams do during a night's sleep,
sometimes never reaching the port,

but like a ship's manifest drawn up by
a wise seaman who has an accurate
 mental compass inside his mind,

or a poet who consults his dreamy mind
and sends the port up into the clouds
and gives the ship wings
to float along with them,
taking the real and romanticizing it,
sending it into a dream that inspires and
sends you into the clouds with the ship,

nightly dreams inside his head
working during the daylight hours,
taking him to his imaginary port,
but maybe none at all,
maybe casting him adrift for evermore,
or maybe giving the port arms to
pull the ship to the dock and a
welcoming voice to wish him good luck,

stories in dreams, romanticizing the real,
giving it a new name,

coloring it with pastel colors,
rebelling against the prosaic,
freeing up the inhibitions,
and releasing them into the wild,

the truth adorned and given wings
while the truth be known and in the grasp

Rainbows in the Pen

Words sewn together with vibrant colors
with sinewy threads among all others

splashing upon the parchment in ardent haste
running wild like lovers in sweet embrace

pulling the colors from the rainbows down
from high in the sky then to earthen bound

to the eyes, to the heart, to the poetic mind
emptying the skies and leaving none behind

fitting all of heaven inside one solitary pen
and coating it with the finest colors then

melting them down in the furnace in the soul
stoking the fires with a mysterious exotic coal

heating up the heart with yellows and reds
tying words together with flaming threads

moving the pen through jungles and exotic isles
to the dens of vixens and exposing all her wiles

coloring life with roses and sweet perfumes
living up high and lounging in blue rooms

as the pen travels from spectrum to spectrum
with rainbows and threads so tightly spun

writing sonnets with colors that dance
that move ahead and through time advance.

For words are rainbows and colors written down,
that spill upon the parchment so tightly bound.

Prelude to a Poem

Prelude to a poem, rhyming rivers flowing
 around the bends in an effervescent glowing

and in silken chutes from heaven's doors,
sliding upward and down to earthen floors,

into auditory caves from melodic streaming
and oceans of rapture with spirits beaming

announcing the coming of an exotic sound
of words melted down and spread all round

into stories that lift the spirit into the clouds
that rides with the wind above the earthly crowds

that singes the skin from volcanic fires
and brings to the ears the demonic choirs

or a gentle lullaby that soothes the anxiety
that sends you adrift on a glassy sea

a story that stays with you every day
that mothers you and shows you the way

from a prelude dressed up in ceremonial flair
waving its banners in the quixotic air

sweetened by the spices of exotic gardens
a potpourri of scents and aromatic blends

a fanfare to the threshold of an uplifting paradise
a fire ignited to spread and melt the ice

a prelude leading to a forthcoming poem
a golden avenue to your new poetic home
oh sweet prelude, oh sweet prelude

The Other World

Poets of the real and of the other world
with reality rolled up inside to be unfurled,
reach out to let the other world come to him
and feel it creeping through the fissures in his skin,

into the rivers of his heart and around the bends,
 into iridescent waterfalls and Utopian gardens,
and feel them touching the walls of his stolid heart,
coming inside with torches to burn away the dark,

finding the hidden words that took residence inside,
that piled up and hid to soon take him on a ride,
to sprout wings and fly to other worlds unknown,
 landing in an exotic paradise to call his own,

Oh paradise, how he longs to feel thy texture,
its internal song as in a symphonic overture,
its softness as in a feathered cloud on high,
and its glow melting all the words into a sigh.

An ode to the other world as it drifts about
out of reach but close enough to hear a shout,
and when that shout becomes an earnest plea,
it will come and set his spirit free.

Poetry in the Clouds

The calm rolling across the azure firmament
elevated sighs and images of heaven sent
breath of the Gods in half-way ascension
in picturesque settings for your attention

images of peace and peaceful stories
 by the poets in skyborne inspirited glories
fire heated snowballs drifting in space
puffed up by the lungs of a behemoth race

images of a poetic life in the poetic world
of the glamor of words and rhetoric unfurled
the loosening of wrapped up anxious thoughts
drifting and dreaming and untying the knots

the pen of the clouds dipped in liquid velvets
 and quiet flamencos and silent castanets
clamor becoming less until sound is just a sigh
a poem about the laziness of the quiet sky

a lullaby that drifts and sings to the earth
that melts the jagged cliffs since their day of birth
a portrait of the history of the earth and skies
with colors that circulate through the vivid highs

of imaginary shapes that become real to the poets
the ones who ride upon the quixotic sunsets
and wallow upon the clouds in dreams
and swim in the poetic streams
drifting, floating, singing, riding,
running, flying and - - - - - - - -

The Push

My two worlds too far apart
 drift further away from each other
with each passing hour
with my mind still in the material world
of weights and measures, sinking into vacuity,
longing to see into the other world
that keeps pulling away from me.

Oh music for my summoning, come to me.
Shine your beacons onto my other world.
Let me see what I've been missing.
Let them reach into the fertile gardens
that run deep into the hinterland.
Bring thy richest harmonies and let them
 push me with their sturdy arms
up to my forsaken world that left me behind.
Let the music spread its wings and carry me
past the shores and into the sweet gardens
where I can smell the roses and the jasmine
and look into the beauty that soothes my eyes
that reminds me of what my other world is like.

Give me the words to write so I can see clearer.
I will see them dancing in my dreams,
rubbing their velvet skin against my skin,
running down my spine and into my heart,
floating with my tears that
fall upon the parchment

and don't leave until my poem is finished
and until my heart quivers when I read it again.

Thank you music with thy
 sturdy and poetic arms
for pushing me into my other world
and keeping me there until
my poem was finished.

Precious Rhyme

Words dipped in the waters of poetic bliss
 flowing in rapture as in a lover's kiss
through velvet pipes down Melodic Avenue
swirling toward heaven for a spatial rendezvous

words chosen from deep within the soul
the inner domain of the heart's primal glow
shedding light upon the corridors of thought
of all that was found and all that was taught

a new language that flows through the air
on the wings of poetic rhyme and verbal flair
that come and go and swirl with the wind
to lovers and poets in melodic discipline

a rhyme not like the rigid rules of rhyme
but an easing up along the constricted spine
a natural romp in the lazy clouds aloft
as poets sink into a bewitching trough

a magnet that pulls all thinkers into a maze
up into the deepest space as the sky child plays
as he places these words inside his dizzy mind
and laughs at him and the rest of his kind

poets becoming poets as the tension goes away
words melted into liquid as the fires stay
torches staying lit through the cold and dark
as the fervor and the thoughts come to never part

an ode to life and in the living in it that way
for as long as the fire stays lit and the rhythms sway
precious words swirl about in his poet mind
lifting him up on his poetic climb
words are like ladders up to the highest mount

Passion Engine

A never-ending spark that pushes the pistons
that take the mind and soul
into dark mazes, over hurdles, through walls,
jumping over reason and sensibility,
rising with the heat of lust and carnality,

wild pulses of the savage heart
in obedience to the voices in the loin
with desire overpowering abstinence,
passion overpowering reason
with an end result that bypasses all
the steps that lead to the end
with an urge to climb without a ladder,

or a never-ending spark that
pushes the pistons that
take the mind and spirit to the
gratification of accomplishment,
that climbs the ladder of reason,
gluing the mind to the foreseeable end
while riding on the wings
of pure obstinacy
like hunger leading all creatures to food,
jumping over fences and jagged cliffs,
running with the certainty of time
and calculating each step taken
as the goal becomes a reality and
not just a dream
as dreamers did when they began their climb,

submitting themselves to the passion engine
that drove them to where they wanted to be.

Praise be to the passion engines.
Praise be to the dreamer
that fires them up.
Praise be to the obstinacy
that keeps them going
and praise be to the fire
that never dies.

Spirit Engines

Pistons cranking in the chasms of the soul
spirits in contention for supreme control
churning in the hearts of the hot-blooded warriors
battle songs from the mouths of the infernal whores

engines steaming ahead at supersonic speeds
as combatants mount their spirited steeds
brandishing their swords to follow their command
from the commanders of the highest fatherland

to gain control is the thought on their minds
spreading the heat as the battle climbs
 a stronghold gained in a smoldering fortress
the beast has landed and morality suppressed

or morality cranking at the speed of light
to see the dismantling in the devil's blight
his armies retreating and his voices waning
his laughter muffled and his temper flaming

his feet unsteady in the shifting sand
and his supremacy weakening in all the land
as he falls to the ground to never rise up again
from the churning of the holiest spirit engine

the common man at war with the two spirits
finding his place among his favorites
to let his pleasure choose the one for him
or the righteous one from the divinity within.

Guru Baby

Guru baby with your mini fingers flying
around the keyboard, typing and crying,
computer guru pooping in your diapers
dance around as do all dancing typers.

Goo goo ga ga of high intelligence,
royal baby of highfalutin eminence,
too high up to say how you do it,
can't stop and explain it bit by bit.

Slow down and teach us what you do.
Remember we told you how to tie your shoe.
If you over us try to exercise your power,
you have to go to your room for one whole hour.
If you computer baby let it go to your head,
you have to stay there until it's time to go to bed.

Guard Cows

Watch out!! Beware!! for the hills thou shalt run,
Attack cows on the loose to get you son;
guarding the perimeter of the farmer's yard,
coming to get you and hit you hard.

They run like hell with their tongues hanging out
to lick you with that funky slime about.
They corral you with love on their erotic mind
and lick you with that funky smelling slime,

that funky goo mixed in with some cow bung grass
and you their soul mate still in their grasp,
a horror story you wouldn't wish for your enemy,
an attack cow encounter, a slime drench, a catastrophe.

Lions and tigers, drunken hyenas and killer frogs;
they eat you up like a troupe of skinny hogs.
Your life is over without the stench of slime
mixed in with the cow bung grass funk combined.

So if thou comest upon a farmer's yard,
look for attack cows and look hard,
for they have romance on their minds
and you are their romancee
about to get drenched in slime.
YUK yuk agh——————————
 Getting eaten by a drunken hyena
is better than that.

The Pure the Wild

The pure the wild of passion's blend
  waters of the Styx and the child again
paradise lost and something new
lost in the heat of the witch's brew

charging buffalos and lambs united
raging savages and children incited
to war with battle axes and make-believe toys
fun in the darkest night for all the boys

commanding voices ringing through their ears
listening to their hearts and losing all the fears
rising to the pinnacle of their carnal desires
all what a disciple of the dark prince requires

angels and demons riding through the dark
on the soiled wings of a blood stained lark
chanting battle cries through the perilous night
flexing their muscles for a glorious fight

the pure into the wild, the wild, the wicked
 an entry into battle with the proper ticket
a lamb with a taste of blood in his eyes
dancing with the devil in the downward skies
gone with all disciples of the unholy priest
the pure shedding purity, oh thou wild beast.

Wellness Demons

The ongoing battles with the wellness demons
 are the never-ending wars inside humanity.
The inevitable attacks that never stay away
are of the devil's arming itself
 with spears and battle-axes
to go to war with our internal physician,
our God that functions within us through creation.

 It breaks the shell that shelters the spirit of joy
and plucks the strings of the nerve fibers,
spreading its venom rivers throughout
to control human disposition with a surging pain,
breaking their spirit and rendering them hopeless.

The attention thieves come to live in the mind,
setting up their camps and plotting their moves,
becoming the new masters of the spirit,
the new internal physician that
 dominates the days with misery and grief.

The power of our God.
our intrinsic internal physician
who never tires or loses the battle,
who counts the days of our grief and
promises a brighter future ahead,
brings his remedy to us to drink.

Though bitter it tastes,
the bitterness turns to sweetness when

the devil's venom starts to
recede and wellness takes up
residence in the human spirit.
All hail to the Our God physician within.

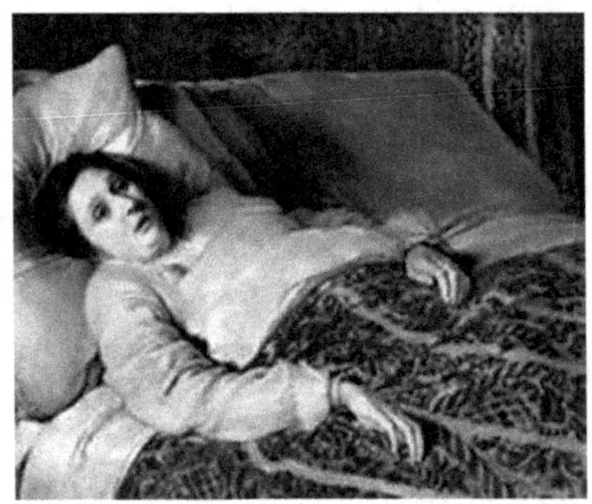

My Unknown of Me

My unknown of me, my blood rivers
winding around and through my body from
divine sources, anointed by the
Grace of God,

rivers soiled from the pure,
stained from the virginal,
rivers in my keeping and maintenance
flowing through delicate channels,
my jungles, my maze, my domain, my haven,
my lost child, my milk, my breath,

being driven by
life longing for itself through
my brittle veins, my palpitating heart,
my flapping valves in constant motion,
pumping life into life, blood into blood,
riding down the rivers of destiny
from divine sources out of my control
from despotic mandates from heaven above,

steady flowing under divine supervision
to destinies unknown,
my other universe, my island
shrouded by the mist
and away from my understanding,

and the beast within me that
screams for dominance,

that battles with the divinity within me
as I weigh my desires with my satisfaction,
pleasure with my abstinence,
my faith with my indecisiveness,
and the me that contains all the elements,

networks of activity within me,
networks controlled by God
and maintained by the both of us
and nourished by my careful vigilance
as life goes on and on and on..........

My Hidden Rivers

My hidden rivers with names I know not,
transporting my life with the proper ingredients,
flowing through my sensitive canals, my veins
with the power to determine my destiny,
my fragile life at the mercy of its flowing,

my blood, my mother, my prayers, my hope,
my God, my liquid temples,
my world that I cannot touch,
the truth that I am that I know nothing about,
the me that is me that I cannot reach
and the God that directed the course
in charge of the flowing,
who created me and whose works
determine my life and death,

rivers that flow through unknown places,
supplying nutriment to these places,
sustaining itself until my final breath,
physicians of the ethereal order
working laboriously day and night
in authority of the flowing
and to where it leads to,

a careful design at creation,
something that no human mind
 could ever think of and execute,
a supreme thought put to use
and carried out,

rivers taken for granted but rivers vital,
rivers exercising their supreme authority,
rivers flowing from the mother of life,
primal rivers with eternal dreams
but rivers with inevitable expiration,
known only by their creator
who started the rivers flowing,
my hidden rivers that are
hidden from my knowledge.

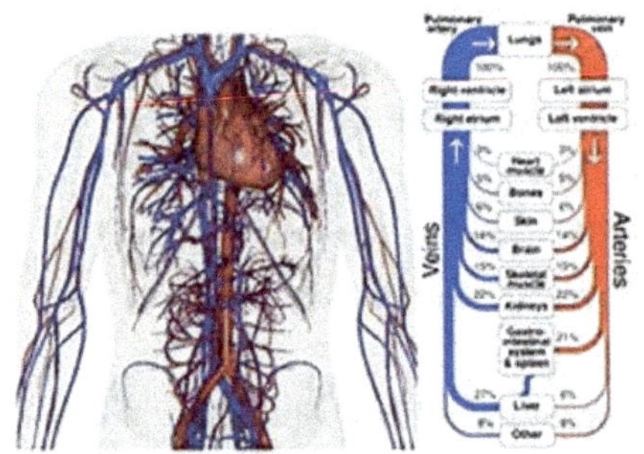

My Private Euphoria

There is a certain chordal structure in all music that fills me with euphoria and not the vast majority. There are other musicians before me with that distinct feeling, because it is there for me to listen to. We are all a part of a very select group that pass on those feelings in our music that only we can be elated from it. Our music idols are musicians that hardly anyone knows. Most everyone can't feel what we can feel.

When I can finally execute a new musical passage or chordal pattern that I heard from them, I can't share my euphoria with most others, because they can't feel what I am feeling. Some say that is wonderful to make me feel good, but it is not wonderful to them. I am alone in my accomplishments.

I can't say it is a handicap, because harmonic advancement is another stage that culture needs to reach in order to be progressive. It is just we, the ones who have to suffer by being misunderstood and not being appreciated for what we did. Popular music took our innovations and used them for its advancement. I feel that our little fraternal group of hypersensitive musicians have been exploited. We invented those chordal structures that they use and make all their money with, and we have many more for them to steal and call their own.

Inside a Dream

Something was floating out in the prosaic air;
an object never seen or heard before,
getting closer as the sound got louder
until it stopped while still suspended in the air.
 I heard it breathing inside a large pliable shell
that expanded with each breath
like a human heart.
It had my name written above the door
like it knew who I was.
With an empathetic, angelic voice it told me to enter.
I stepped inside and looked all around.

Beauty lit up the room and cast away the dark.
It appeared before my eyes and dove into my heart.
It brought poetic words to me that I didn't know.
It put them in my mind and let them flow.

Trees became pliant and started to sing
as the sound blew through and started to ring.
They danced until the wee morning hours
until the opening of the Morning Glory flowers.

Words melted down into a sea of exotic charm.
Poetry and rhyme floated down arm and arm.
They opened up my mind and became so clear
as the words grew wings and flew into my ear.

Heaven dropped down to let me feel its texture,
its supple body and its hallowed smile so pure.

Then after the touch filled me full of sonnets to write,
my heart broke loose and danced into the night.

Then that object that came to me in my dream
flew away and left me wondering.
Maybe it wasn't a dream but
a reality that happened to me.
I am a poet with two minds.
One is locked inside reality
and the other is drifting out into deep space.

Under Lock and Key

More precious than the royal emerald,
or nature's once in a lifetime spectacle,
or the running of the dried-up rivers again,
or the words in my mind without an end,
I keep them sealed under lock and key
in an iron vault under eternity's decree.

Years pile on top of every year from before
like the never-ending rains for ever more,
washing away the words that live inside
as Father Time takes me on a persistent ride
amongst the thieves who take away one more word
as I travel day after day that subsequently occurred.

My mind is my precious tool for my success.
Father Time steals what he can and leaves me with the rest.
I keep them locked up in my iron vault
tightly sealed to form a solid wall.
So when I die I can keep what words remain
and remember so well from whence they came.

Fanfare for my Reverie

Stravinsky's "The Rite of Spring" fills up my mind
and watches my prosaic thoughts unwind,
slowly slipping away like winter's funeral
like a song of joy to its reluctant submittal.

A fanfare with adherent arms that enfold me,
brings me to the scene of springtime's reveille
and places it inside of me to fire up my passion,
the new me, the me that became so venturesome.

I ran with it into the jungles of imagination
with a brand-new feeling and a thrilling sensation.
It loosened up the straps that bind me to myself,
got into my mind through magic and cast a spell.

The new me became a poet of that haunting sound
that echoed through me like empty rooms all around,
but rooms filled up with the scent of rose gardens
that left me with a new spirit and my soul cleansed.

Then the exploding drums drove me into the tempest
through its menacing teeth and into its fiery chest
where I could feel the lightning bolts on a rampage
as I slid down on their backs to my earthen stage.

But it lit my pen on fire as I wrote my poem
and the passion released my spirit to roam;
soft sounds like the touch of a feather,
then hell and dissonance all mixed together.
An ode to Stravinsky's " The Right of Spring"
that brings me to my poem and makes me sing.

The Cradling

In the world outside the wolves run wild,
free to hunt and kill on Savage Isle
where God is God and wolves are wolves,
out to kill as the food chain moves.

Civilization is in the taming yet to be tamed,
and all the beasts become fair game,
and life is a world of running and hiding,
looking for food with fighters fighting.

Peace is a climb up to Gluten's Peak
from the battle of the strong and of the weak,
where God is the guardian of the food chain
and yet the God of love through all the pain.

And mothers are clothed in protective armor
with thorns colored in pink and lavender
and perceptive eyes that look out into the wild
with thoughts on protecting her innocent child.

Mother's gentle arms are so soft and slight
yet strong and able and ready to fight
as she opens them up to cradle her young
and sings a sweet lullaby to her little one.

"Sleep, sleep, sleep, my precious child.
Mother is hear with you all the while
to fight off the wolves with all my might

and cradle you in my arms all day and night.
As you leave someday you can fight on your own;
but today you are safe until you're fully grown.
So sleep, sleep, sleep my precious child.
Sleep, sleep, sleep."

Sunshine Eyes

Her eyes at the end of the tunnel,
her beacon that shows the way out,
out of the darkness that dimmed the spirit of man,
 an alluring light that reaches to the senses,
a flame that warms up their outer layers
and seeps through their hardened shells
that brings on the intoxication of life
and separates it from the awakening,
that opens up the book authored by the
the designer of life,

the first page, the chapter on lust,
a feeling undeniable,
and what it does to the human spirit,
the desire to fully digest it,
the need to feel its presence
 and become intimate with it,
the need to let it roam
through the empty chasms
as it works its way to the loin,

man and woman, man and his needs,
woman and her needs, her mortal fulfillment,
her knowledge of the needs of man,
man beset by a darkness that numbed his senses,
man with his eyes thirsting for beauty,
a beacon that will lead the way out,
common man with common desires,
common man since the Garden of Eden.
Who doesn't feel the way he feels?

My Private Muse

My muse, my inspiration, my whimsical flier,
my hidden gem, my knighted rider,

she with a poem in her bewitching heart
at home in her secret hideaway in the dark,

who keeps heaven's language locked up inside
to give to me on her midnight ride,

who swirls about with the winds from up high
and then swoops down to somewhere nigh,

somewhere for me to find, somewhere I know not,
somewhere that she chose to be her landing spot,

my private muse who loves to tease,
who hovers above my mind, then gets up and leaves,

and laughs as she goes home to the poet gods
then rides back down on the lightning rods.

 If I could see her flying above the mountain crest,
I could catch her and sit her down at my desk.
I could write the most beautiful poem ever written.
I could feel the words from my heart so smitten.
I could rise above and live in her palace.
I could taste her wine and drink from her glass.
I could become intoxicated and write about it.
I could speak the language of her spirit.

I could make her all mine to stay forever,
to give me words that make my body quiver.
I could, I could, I could, I could.

The Luring

Beauty with her glistening about
her aura heating up the cold
her face melting away the ice
her fires shooting through her eyes
her blood boiling in the beholder's veins
her magnetic charm pulling in all and all
her hair of ebony rivers flowing
her smiles smoothing out the rigid air
her warmth exuding and circulating
her furnaces fired up and running
her heated oils accentuating her skin
her glossy flesh glowing in the sun
her slender arms caressing the wind
her walks suspended above the floors
her feet dipped in perfume and exotic spices
her movements of charm and grace
 her mouth an adit to her hallowed caves
her spirit running through the veins
her voice a rhapsody of the winds
her words penned by the poets
her language sanctified by the saints
her beauty beyond all beauty

her tantalizing unassumed and overlooked
her modesty wrapped up in her innocence
her thoughts blooming from pure gardens
her beauty melting all human hearts
her aura filling them up with exotic spices

her luring beyond all magnetic forces
her pulling in of kings and priests
her toying with humanity but
not for the sake of toying
her beauty unexplained but
powerful and compelling
and coveted by all

Sally and her Boy Toys

Sweet little Sally playing with her dolls,
her mommies and daddies and all her animals
and boys and girls being moved up and down
in her pretty pink doll house in and around,

making her cute little dolls obey her commands
and moving their arms and legs and hands
and talking to them like mommy talks to daddy
before bedtime in a language strange and savvy,

sweet little Sally unaware of what the future will bring,
when her womanly curves can make the big boys sing,
and what daddy does to mommy behind the doors,
when they are quiet up until they shake the floors,

sweet little Sally now a big girl in tight dresses,
surprised by all the charm that she now possesses,
how she can bring the boys around to play,
as she raises her skirts and tells them to stay,

then telling them to go until it's time to come again
as she lowers her skirts and wears a big grin,
knowing she has the power to make them obey,
 to make them fall in love, then tells them to go away.

sweet little Sally, not so sweet anymore,
playing with her dolls like she did before,
and turning them into slaves to obey her commands
as vixens do by sticking to their plans,

sweet little Sally, going out into the world,
raising up her skirts to give the boys a whirl
as she plays with her collection of boy toys
she does what she does to bring her all the joys.

Whores do it for a business to make a hefty treasure.
Sally does it to toy with the intensity of pleasure.

Adrenalin Candy

Oh, the sweetness of the surging rivers,
the way they feel as the body quivers,
the thrilling ride to the highest peak,
the heart and soul ecstatic as they beat,

sweet adrenalin pounding against the walls
and fire in the hollows when danger calls,
life and death running through the heart,
reasoning and abstinance yet miles apart,

ode to the feeling and to the glory of the rush
and life as it kisses death with a rousing brush
as it climbs up the spine and into the spirit
and into danger with no reason to fear it.

Oh sweet adrenalin waiting to make a move,
to find my fearful me and put me in a groove
and push me to where I want to go,
to Fool's Paradise or Morality's Flow.

This New Pleasure

Surging rivers reaching every crevasse of my being,
alien waters from an exotic island,
hot and cold lava splashing against the walls,

fires of love invading my being,
slamming against the banks with iron feathers,
massaging my caves with dissonant melodies,
music and spears from another universe,
another being inside my being,
another fragrance, another pleasure, another clime,

a rolling down my spine with jagged wheels,
a velvet pounding, a soothing onslaught,
a volcanic outburst, a feathery drifting
on lilting clouds and tempest furor,

love's sweet pounding with perfumed fists,
ambrosial highlands above my virgin nostrils
planting new gardens in my tender groin,
my virginal rivers filling up with exotic herbs,
my new being exploding with fragrant flowers,
mysterious torches burning a hole in my chest,
new pleasures invading my virgin fields,

my armies submitting to their intoxicating power,
my legs turned to rubber and feeble trees,
and me with no name and no home,
taken by the wind up to the exotic highlands,

to another home in the floating clouds,
the me transformed and given a new name,

a victim of love, a virgin nomad, a man possessed,
a man with rubber legs, a man afloat,
adrift on the high seas,
being blown by the wind to a new paradise,
a drifter with a breath of love in the sails
without a care of the world left behind,
filled with this new pleasure in his being.
Oh, to the power of love and love's consummation.

The Winds of Ambrosia

The sweet winds of ambrosia blew through me,
given birth in the rose gardens from the Isle of She.

The winds from mounds of roses pilled a mile high
 muted my speech and became to me just a sigh.

I captured the aroma of heaven inside my chasms
and felt the wings from the flight of the Seraphims.

They brushed against my cheek and into my senses,
opening up my prisons and tearing down the fences.

She walked past me, through me, and into my being
as the abandoned singer within me got up to sing.

Exotic melodies were flowing through my rivers
with skies full of rose colored and herbal lavenders.

Guitars with the strings of the rainbow sounding
ran through me as my heart was pounding.

They took me into the flight of the ambrosial winds
where I could feel her air as my resurrection begins.

My feet are off the ground and my name is gone,
gone away with my forgotten self and beyond.

I'm in her Paradise looking for her to appear again,
enchanted and forgotten for a hundred years and ten.

 Her wind stays inside me and won't come out
 as I wait for her from all her swirling about.

The Beguiling

Heaven embodied and heaven distorted
evil schemed and evil transported

 a Goddess formed and a Goddess employed
a sacrilege performed and a devotion destroyed

Her of angelic speech and magnetic eyes
flimsy red dresses and flashing thighs

beauty as a beacon and beauty as a tool
 she's beauty on a mission to find a fool

virgins swirling round and round in her vision
from their mothers' arms to a careless collision

a love entanglement caught in a spider's web
a virgin adventure in a temptress bed

a beguiling that took away his identity
a boy that became a broken man to pity

as she moves away and looks for another
with her open thighs for him to smother

a lesson learned for this little man
stand up for yourself and make a plan

The She of Passion

The she of no name but heated oceans
a den of desire and electric potions
a heated pit of love and love's calling
ambrosial gardens and skies of falling

a passion drawn by magnets and spice
a trip to the sacred gardens and lovely vice
a sensual compulsion and forfeit of the mind
a blinding journey and the absence of time

a desire to stay in the sea of no return
to drown and let the waves churn and churn
to feel the feeling and let it last
centuries into centuries into oceans vast

a weightless drifting into an exotic paradise
a perilous adventure and a willing sacrifice
to dive into love as love's sacred feast
and feel the heat from love's erotic beast
with she of no name over her heated door
 lost at sea with no boundaries nor shore

Air of Passion

Mystic crimson-colored engines
hidden in the air but prominent in the groin,
pumping passion through ambrosial channels,
dancing between two lovers and
 inviting them to the dance,
swirling their graceful arms to the
rhythm of the poetic air,

 and despotic engines with their utmost strength
pulling them into a realm of oblivion,
stealing their identity and self-awareness,
injecting them with an aphrodisiacal potion
that fleets directly to the groin
and drags them to the dance,

and engines pumping new feelings in them,
engines manned by the rebels of abstinence
who break the rules of courtship and romance,
who fly through the air with their vile wings
laughing at the Gods of Divinity,
spreading their own truths
about the morality of lust,
ever finding lovers to fill
the air between them
and intoxicate them with their magic potions,
those ancient sorcerers who invaded the
the Sacred Garden and who will outlive us all,

and those engines that resurrect our senses,
that raise us up to our own awareness,
that speak to the ear of our hearts,
that consecrate our pleasure that
we knew nothing about,
and who will ever fill the air
with an extreme exhilaration.

Fire Song

Torches burning through the melodic night
parting the heavy air with all their might

yellow flames dancing as in a spirited sunrise
dressing up the night with an effervescent guise

bringing heat to the solemn corridors
finding its way through the narrow pores

down into the heart and slumbering limbs
a fanfare to the spirit as the music begins

a fire to burn away the catacombs of the dead
and from their resurrection they climb up ahead

they shall dance with the fire in their heated loins
through the night 'til when the morning joins

fire song blazing oh beautiful blaze
melody stuffed with heat and indomitable craze

to the highest peak thou shalt soar
and to the deepest jungles to open the door

and to the wilds they reach their fate
with a fire song for them to captivate

Penetrating Eyes

Penetrating eyes, emphatic oceans,
slavers of the drifting seafarers,
dominating beacons shining brightly
with eyes of steel and feathers and insight
in volumes of mystery and wonder,
vibrating stories filling up the abyss,
hurling spears at the outer walls
as the blazing tips illuminate the insides,
reaching into the heart of the senses,
looking for instantaneous reflections,
bringing out the tears and euphoria,
the inside reaching the surface,
revealing all the deep-seated truths,

as puppeteers pull the strings,
manipulating the senses of total wonder,
the magic of sight and feelings in bloom,
spears of the eyes piercing the heart,
casting steadfast convictions into slavery,

penetrating eyes becoming despotic masters,
an enchantress pulling in all the lovelorn
enchanted by their magnetic powers,
of beauty with its fragrant arms
and tender feet,
eyes empowered by sorcery and fire
riding upon lightning bolts,
splitting the clouds with their teeth
and spraying them with their smoke,

penetrating eyes burning holes in the sun,
dancing in the moonlight and moving the tides,
tightening the straps that hold the earth together
and surging ahead with their magical power,
out and about and moving into forever............

He-man Proof Bottle Caps

Heave-ho he-man of he-man might,
twist and turn and fight fight fight.
Bottle caps are made for babies to twist
and baby rental agencies are here to assist.

Before you smash the bottle against the wall
and run naked through the streets and all,
or kick the dog and piss on the cat,
rent a baby to figure how to turn the cap.

Baby proof bottle caps are baby toys,
fun fun fun for tiny girls and tiny boys.
They can bang on them til they all fall off
and watch them falling down so soft.

Or if you can't get a hold of a super duper baby,
then you can use dynamite to set it free.
If they can open the bottle with their banging
then TNT will do the job without failing.

The proper solution is to never get sick,
 and never call upon babies to do the trick.
Sometimes maybe they won't be there
so you'll just kick the bucket anyway unaware.

If thou art a soon to be kick the bucketer
then suicide is the best solution for the better.
Medicine bottles caps are too complicated

and with no babies around, you just can't wait.
So it's good by cruel world and
you cruel medicine bottle cap makers.
You are among the worst of all my haters.

A Tail Named Fido

A tail named Fido wagging its dog,
happy in the sun and happy in the fog,
dances to the polka, round and round
 to a dizzy round about on the ground.

The sound of a dog banging against the wall
 is a hound tightly wound like a basketball.
 They bounce and hop like some drunken frogs,
as happy tails pounce and wag their dogs.

To teach a tail to sit up and speak
is a job and a half in a year and a week
as Fido wags his dog to get a treat,
"Good tail Fido you done good to me."

Tails that wag their dogs are rare this day
and tails that do tricks, hip hip hurray.
Fido is amoung the best with his tricks,
wagging his dog at half past six.
Hurray for Fido as he wags his dog.

Passion Fire

The need to employ the talent within
with the team losing 101 to 99,
time for the last minute three pointer,
 the summoning to the arsenal deep inside,
the reaching down to the idle engines,
filling them with fuel to enliven them,
to make them prance and kick their feet
and empower them to use the strength
to pull them through Dante's ordeal,

to gather up the kindling wood
in preparation for the passion fire,
the ignition of the flame to drive the pistons,
to fuel the passion and send it surging
through the incendiary veins of the
 intricate human network
in the body of man as the rivers of adrenaline
shall send the ball at the hoop
and good fortune will steer it through
as the God within works in his spirit,
giving him the talent and helping him to execute it.

Up through the blessed air the ball sails,
the same air anointed by the grace of God.
His hopes are written on his distorted face
as the ball nears the center of the rim.
His whole body smiles with that desperate shot
as it sails through the hoop with

him sailing with it with his pride
written all over his face.

His spirit grew wings to lift him up.
It brought him up to be with
the ancient spirits of the Roman Emperors,
the conquistadors of the seas,
and the ghosts of the departed champions
while he pranced and danced on earth
from his job well done.
Good game Mr. DiVincenzo.

Rain Pain

Rain pain and spirits head downward
 to the darkened cellars along melancholy boulevard
with only half of the upward skies in view
and heaven shielded by a thickened grayish hue.

Seeking dominance over God's eternal realm,
only the shadows of God take over the helm,
and the worshipers are cheated by the dark haze
as the rains come down from a broken praise.

Each drop of rain carries an uplifting message
as the emptying of the clouds fulfill their pledge,
and the view of heaven becomes more clear
as the empyreal opens up above the hemisphere.

At last, the celebratory feast of the hungry daffodils,
the dancing in the meadows and upon the hills
take place as the flowers begin to bloom
from pieces of the clouds so salutarily strewn.

And the Earth begins to sing summer's song
about how joy and sorrow come along,
and sorrow strengthens the way for the rain to fall
when despair is averted, and gladness is installed.

The philosophy of life is inside one little rain drop
while the mind is crying for it to stop.
And the knowing of its effect is in the wisdom,
the strength that builds through the pandemonium
as the rain pain eases up and the anguish subsides.

Nocturnal Fires

Lofted wars of the restless skies,
upward hell risen from pacific grounds,
infernal fires from the demonic cannons
or spectral fires from the ghosts of the Apocalypse,
or blitzes born from the spasmodic militants
from their homes in the complicated skies,
the skies controlled by two minds,
the peaceful that sings in the blooming of the roses
or the disquieted ones that ride on a lightning bolt,
opening their hearts to the thrill of the ride
with one mind claiming victory over the other,
where nocturnal fires erupt from their conquest
over the splintered trees and charred forests
that were in the wake
 from the war of evil over the good,

but such beauty in the deeds of the evil,
the animated galleries moving through the restless air,
the midnight flashing, the spasmatic impulses,
the bright colors shimmering against the black sky,
the jagged knives slicing through the black clouds,
nocturnal fires and their skyline illuminations,
the sweet rumbling of the saccharine skies,
the crackling sounds of the lightning
like a team of tympani blasting away in the
 prelude to the grand finale of an animated opus,
a rousing rhythm with an accelerating volume
that brings the orchestral piece to a glorious ending,

and a waking up the stagnant spirit that goes to sleep
during the lengthy calming that is too calm,
the days too quiet, the nights too placid,
the air too lethargic, the vanishment of the clouds,
the Earth searching for a pulse,
a glimmer of rebellion, a stirring uprising,
a revolt against the dominating stagnation
that numbed the spirit in the human heart
and cast humanity into a deep sleep.

"Oh, skies of good and evil,
please go to war again and chase away the
cobwebs that settled down in the human spirit."

Virgin Navigation

Waters of the primal clouds so pure
like the birth of a symphonic overture

a high thought by the God up above
up above the flight of a sky-bound dove

the clashing of the winds so hot and cold
as the nervous clouds begin to roll

an omnipotent intelligence as a foundation
composing a system for a reliable navigation

a simple result of a master plan executed
of the lazy stubborn air being uprooted

a forming of the virgin waters to fall down
through the readied skies to the virgin ground

as virginal at birth and pure as a mother's milk
and woven as soft as the finest silk

losing its virginity as it sinks into the earth
seeping into the ground with spunk and mirth

then mixing in with the old impure waters
under the authority of their botanical fathers

nutrients for the grapes in the healthy vineyards
and the grasses and flowers in the manicured yards

from virgin skies to clouds to virgin navigation
to the falling and to the subsequent vegetation

as life longs for itself through a complex system
from our Master of creation, again and again.

Chameleon Clouds

Clouds change from the rising sun
 into the sunset from their day on the run,
and colors bleed into colors
like chameleons just like their shifting mothers.

Nature's a painter with an iridescent eye
at the easel looking out at the inconsistent sky,
the moving waves of the drifting clouds
and the colors they keep as they stop to browse.

Beauty is in the sunrise as the day begins
and in the sunset according to earthly disciplines.
She changes colors that enchant the heart
and keeps the rage from coming apart.

 Clouds are like chameleons with colors that shift.
They float up above the hills and forever drift.
They are like a kaleidoscope that never settles down,
changing colors and keeping off the ground.

I looked to the sky this morning and lo behold
a purple cloud that changed to gold.
And then the sun moved in a westward direction.
Then it turned red before the sun kissed the ocean.
Then the cloud turned black beyond my sight
and became a mystery of the cryptic night.
Yes there is magic in the skies there is.

Thunder Torches

Torches cutting trails in the nighttime skies
lighting up the darkness in a lovely disguise

of beauty flaunted and beauty impassioned
passion released and taken to the end

cracking through the perforated clouds
in proud submission to its wicked vows

 from the dark prince at his demonic altars
on a mission to burn and split the stars

to light up the sky and show the devil's works
and twisted ladies dancing in rising skirts

 fired up torches aiming at the highest trees
in cadence to the thunder as it swiftly leaves

such beauty in the sky, a gallery of passion
the birth and life of the tempest in action

from the gentle skies to the house of the savage
the running of the course of a tumultuous rage

lightning bolts shot out of diabolic cannons
from the sorcery of the sorcerer's wands

a vengeance against the air that tranquilized the earth
the air that was sanctified at its sacred birth

the air made unholy as the fire ran through
soiled from the boiling of a witch's brew

the running of the passion of the thunder torches
as it touches, as it singes, then until it scorches

beautiful, illuminated skies, lightning dances,
power drumming, power unleashed, power supreme,
Thunder Gods singing, earth shaking,
oh yes, the gallery of the tempest,
the glamour of the heated skies
on a mission of demolition upon the earth.

Virgin Rains

In the upward skies
on the way to the highest home,
the sacred kingdom, home of the blessed,
where the clouds mark the boundaries
 of the air that is split into two segments,
the pure abyss and the soiled earthly part,
the division where the cold mingles with the hot
and where the clouds lounge about the skies
loading up themselves with virgin waters
anointed with the wand of the highest priest,
drawn from the wells of the drifting cathedrals,
the rain forms and readies itself for its descent.

Down, down, down through the earthly sky
it brings the ambiance of the upper skies into view,
the anointed waters of the highest priest
 that loses its purity for a good cause,
the moistening of the dusty fields below
on a mission to answer the pleas
of the forsaken farmers.

Oh, virgin rains, giver and sustainer of life,
mercy of the sympathetic heavens,
tears of the consecrated clouds,
purifier of the impure earth,
cleanser of the squalid skin,
supplier to the feeble rivers,
empowering them to run to the seas
and return to the skies with
intentions of falling again in due time,
please do not ever stop thy forming and falling.

Battle Air

Smoke fills up the feeble valleys,
the Eden Gardens, the skin of the most holy,
the lakes of purity, the baptismal waters,
the face of the emerald earth
 with the air from the northern battlegrounds
where nature went to war with herself,
her evil that lives deep down in the
chasms of Gomorrah at war with the
divinity that reigns over her emerald gardens,
 the pure air that fills the lungs of the blessed,

her burning timbers lashing out at the
beauty of the clean faces of the divine order,
marring the saintly skin that watched over it
as she spread her wrath about the land,
her parched fields vulnerable to the ire of the
blazing sun and the wayward winds
igniting her trees that she built up
through the long years and now
reduced to smoldering embers that mar the
beauty of the vibrating forests,

the smoke penetrating the southern lands,
moving over the succulent fields,
drifting with the winds that guide it along
as if the winds were the works of
the prince of darkness from the evil side
that festers in her soul,
the conflicts that she thinks her way into

as she builds up her opposing armies from within,
just like humanity at war with itself,
building up their armies to
fuel the deeds of their opposing destinies.

But Mother Nature always seems to atone
for her malicious deeds with the rains
that come just in time to quench the fires
and supply the nitrogen from them
that sinks into the soil to resurrect the latent fields.
So what do we humans do about our malicious deeds?

The Explosion

Below the tranquil banks looking at the sea,
the power of the waves and of the solid rocks
create a foam of white flowers
 as they explode and
reach into the air with their frothy arms,
posing as if time was an illusion
and the earth stopped its eternal pulse
and the immobile sun hung in the mystic sky.

The white flowers stuck out their proud chests
with their feet still glued to the water,
their electric eyes aiming at the shore,
their smiles dipped in honey,
 their whiteness glistening in the sun,
picture perfect, portrait of heaven,
milk of sainted mothers, of pure clouds,
skin of velvet textures and tears of angels,
breaking up into fragments of oceanic lore
as they bring in the secrets of the deep beyond,
the mother lode of the intensive divers,
dashing against the stubborn muted rocks
and then returning again
back into the calm as if the sea
was made of glass and the mystery
remained forever a mystery.

Oh beautiful white flowers posing in the air;
thou art the lore of the deep blue sea
and the sunken paradise before mine eyes.
Be forever more as thou art now.

Heyday of the Saga

A lucky star shined down on Jake today.
It broke through the perforated clouds
that hovered over the Bering Sea
and found him in deep thought.
It entered into his eyes and
 filtered down to his apprehensive heart.
It gave him the courage to move ahead.
It stayed with him as he took over
the captain's cabin of the Saga.
It smoothed over the Bering Sea for him.
It illuminated the waters deep within.
It pointed out where the schools were and
 told the Cod Fish to assemble for him.
It told him to trust in its findings
and to be obedient to its credibility.
It told him when to lower the pods
and gathered up the fish for him.
It put a gladness in the hearts
of the fishermen as they hoisted up
the pods full of fish, one after another.

As the numbers surmounted,
so did the money.
That special day was
a heyday for Jake along with
the rest of the days
and the crew leading up to
a prosperous season.
Thanks be to that lucky star.

Fanfare to the Tempest

The quiet strings smoothed out the restless tide,
and everything sat still with an emptiness inside.
The soggy air hung above the glassy water
and the quiet grew soft and the soft grew quieter.
Hush-h-h-h-h-h-h-h-h-h.

Sound the trumpets, the fanfare to the tempest,
the pounding tympani at an urgent request,
the picollos screaming up higher and higher,
up to the highest seagull and nautical flier,

trumpeteers with TNT inside the valves
rousing sleepers and boosting their morales,
aimed at the teeth of the swirling clouds
with thunder booming from open mouths,

a fanfare for all charging lightning bolts
with all the power of a million volts,
triple fortissimo and louder if it can be,
louder than the cracking as seagulls flee.

Here come the tempest and it do come
with all the pomp and blasting drum,
bringing on the fury of the stormy waters
and rousing up the old Neptune's daughters.

The tempest do come, do come alright,
with missiles and spears and ready for the fight.
WAKE UP YOU IDLE SEAFARERS YOU!

Heated Waters

Heated waters, arsenals of the Swirling Beast,
gracious hosts for an up-and-coming lavish feast,
paradise for the hurricanes that come to dinner,
are readying their speech to proclaim the winner.

Lazing upon the glassy troughs and crests
in obedience to the dreaded tempest's request,
they heat up as the sun casts its searing rays
in accordance with the hotter summer days.

Tempers scorching and shedding the cool about
festering in the soul for a forthcoming heated bout
with spears in the winds and swords in the water
they send the ships and the crew to a certain slaughter.

When all ashore is luxuriating in summer's green,
the oncoming tempest comes to spoil their dream.
With razor teeth and hostility in their breath
they swoop in to inflict a certain death.

Prepare ye shipmates for a stormy ride
as the waters grow hot and burn up the tide.
Batten down the hatches and prepare for war
for the overpowering dreaded Conquistador,
proclaiming in the troughs of the stormy sea,
"The ocean that was yours belongs to me."

Summer Snows

Off in the distance on top of the hill
above the sun-baked pine trees,
 the late afternoon sun splashes against the
silken white alabaster clouds that ride along,
floating in the crispy summer skies
against the dark blue firmament
in the gallery in the eyes of the beholder.

Winter snows that cover the hills
in the heat of summer
in their deceiving magic
 enter into the picture as the
 unassuming virgin clouds
 dressed in a white chiffon
with silver wheels slowly churning,
move in a poetic manner like a hurricane
as seen from high above it;
its rare beauty seen only for a moment
until the nocturnal blanket covers them up
as they sleep in peace through the night.

Goodby clouds in the crispy skies,
a lullaby for the sensations gone by,
the falling of the lofted dreams,
the helium seeping out of them,
the touchdown upon the earth,
back to the grind of life with
the anxious anticipation to see them again,
back to the drama of the prosaic skies,

a poem without the air to breathe,
a song without harmony to keep it afloat,
and a blanket to cover up the poetic skies.

Come back again
and massage my anxious heart
and give me the words to write,
the words that abandoned me
when nighttime fell and
took away my inspiration.

Pennsylvania Rains

Prayers in the dusty fields of corn
where the farmers weep and wonder
if the world is drying up or shifting,
if there ever will be the rains again,
what it feels like against their searing skin,
if the crops will ever be again
lunging through the loam
and rising up toward the sun in their
vibrant green suits holding their palms
upward to receive the rains that soak
 the grounds from whence they arose.

"Oh beautiful, sweet, savory, luscious,
succulent, cooling, heroic rains,
why hast thou forsaken us?"

Clouds of mercy and clouds of compliance,
reparations of the Rain Gods made,
atoning for the sins of the complacent air
where the hot and cold fronts stay away,
snuggled inside their own separate island,
hanging inside the tired old firmament
at peace with each other like a
lioness with her cubs,

at last a restlessness stirring in the pacific air,
a desire to dominate over the other front,
a clashing together of the armies,
an angry tempest forming,

a rumbling of the clouds,
a falling of the rains onto
the dried up fields of corn,

at last the fields of Pennsylvania
 flourished again and rescued
the hungry people as the Rain Gods
made sure to execute their duties
and shed their tears over the land.

The Inversion of Heaven

The inversion of Heaven, a blessed miracle
with earth overhead in a corrupted pinnacle

and heaven below where God is in control
as the high earth sits in its new abode

God as the efficient motivator in all our daily lives
and all the fighting and unrest up high in the skies

far from earthen activities are they up overhead
with their quest for power and to armies led

we earthen citizens satisfied with what we have
and to them in the sky we look up and laugh

lofted fools getting scorched by the blazing sun
and we cooled by the waters that we have swum

we on earth united with God and love
and they united with no one up above

we living as God made us to live
and they all for themselves with nothing to give

But what about life after death, the skyward ascension?
Would it be another inversion?
Or would we suffer with the others up high
and join their armies and to them comply?

And then we would go back to how we were.

Blessed Air Abounding

Blessed air from ancient islands abounding
down from heaven with trumpets sounding

music of the cherubims swirling throughout
as the voice of the angels speak forth and sprout

speaking from pure thoughts with silver tongues
playing with the winds on silent drums

sending sky-built currents into sacred spaces
reserved for gallant saints in consecrated places

high priests assembling for the earthly mission
aligning with the climes in rhythmic precision

taking wings to settle down in stony hearts
residing in peace as the discordance departs

filling up the spaces that hostility once owned
that the dark knight once sat upon the throne

pure air penetrating the lungs and thoughts
oxygen for the hungry heart and tender spots

abounding in the air that we breathe and digest
to purify our hearts from our supplications request

Drink of Life

Oh-h sweet nectar of the medicinal clouds,
pour your fruits upon the withered brows.
Beat upon the fields with thy golden rain
and keep the corn free above the pain.

Send a hearty deluge until the skies are empty.
Fulfill thy duties according to heaven's decree.
Answer the pleas of the forsaken earth
and do this in compliance to thy oath at birth.

Take yourself back to thy time of creation,
on the drawing board as a firm foundation,
when the sky was just an empty space
waiting to be showered with heaven's embrace.

Rain when it is the right time to rain
and when it is enough, 'tis time to refrain.
Keep to the plan of needs and their fulfillment,
managing the duration of the water's descent.

For the drink of life needs just enough
to keep us living for ever and ever more.

Pilots in the Currents

Capricious pilots, slaves of the master currents
in obedience to the shifting winds of indifference

pilots at the helm of the currents in the skies
 seen only by the poets and the mystic wise

weavers of quixotic dreams and aeronautic lore
governed by a supreme power for always evermore

employed when the spirit moved across the waters
before fathers came to be fathers and begotten fathers

pilots, rulers at the half-way ladder to the heavens
up to where the soiled air and the hallowed spirit blends

pilots in the cockpits of the upward streaming tides
watching up and down and over with all three eyes

pilots trained by the authority of the wayward wind
disciples of the Wind Gods as a steadfast discipline

blowing the clouds and moving them at will
colliding with other clouds for a capricious thrill

watching them twist and turn and swirl about
and change colors while moving throughout

Oh pilots in the master currents;
blow the clouds away and make them come back.

Residue from the Attic

Fragments of lower heaven flying in the air
from the attic of the upward skies,
ivory chunks of feathery velvet dancing
with the December winds
in rhythm with the overbearing breath
that circulates through the lower empyrean
and directs the motion of the submissive air,

the air that fills up with the dews of heaven
and builds a willowy citadel as a gray mist
that forms a cloud that spills over
and goes to war in the fields of the tepid air
 claiming its dominance in the unsettled skies,
waving its banners in victory,
the conquistador of the upper region,

yet a force being overpowered by another force,
 being pushed by the rhythms of its breath,
a force softened by the universal power
that controls the positioning of the skies
and the assemblage of the clouds,

December snows cascading down so slowly
dancing under the heavens so holy,
residue of the skyward attic
as Nature's charm and celestial magic,
hymns of the wind through the naked trees,
melodious commands of Supremacy's decrees
as snowflakes fall
so majestic and small.

The Winds of Turmoil

Lazy skies of no spirit or stirring
no sound, no voices, no wind, no whirring,

like dancing with no drums to move along
a lullaby with no dynamics in the tired song

an empty space with nothing to fill it with
an ancient scroll revealing nothing but a myth

winds in the calm of the listless skies
waiting for the finale of the sleepy lullabies

to hear the whirring of the skyborn fans
the dancing clouds above the quiet lands

the swaying barley in the late summer fields
the contentious sky warriors with their battle shields

the assembling black clouds rolling into each other
battle ready voices shouting one after another

 lightning bolts parting the compacted clouds
burning a hole from the fire in their mouths

splitting the proud trees that once were grand
from the fire and water over all the land

the story of the tranquil winds that became restless
born of an angel that became possessed

the story of too many earthly inhabitants
that live to release their addiction to violence

Air of Relevance

Air of relevance, air of the unseen,
giver and sustainer of life,
rising from the dark into prominence,
the hidden authority of the winds,
the hands that are there but not there,
that hold up and propel the butterfly,
that speaks through the cracks in the trees,
that rustles the leaves with soft whispers,
that sings through the bell of the trumpet,
that converts the air into sweet music,
that shapes and molds it with loving breath,
pushing it around the bend of the portals,
breaking down matter into celestial fragments,
notes into prose and prose into music.

Or riding with the breath of the tempest,
the madness running through the sky,
cursing at the passive seas,
laughing at the glassy waters,
assembling the clouds together
in the teeth of the devil,
the blacks, the grays, the risen hell,
the home of the beast, the lofted lair,
the wild land with no laws or civility,
six hundred and sixty six miles from heaven,
an inch away in the vast desert of the skies,
a hell next door to heaven,
a quiet valley resting in the wicked arms
of the wicked beast in the wicked skies,

the monitor of the mood in the air,
the commander of the motion of the clouds,
the tyrant of the earth,
the giver and taker of life,
the relevance of the unseen,
the feel of its touch,
and the perplexity of its movement.

Fires of the Divine

Let there be light on the Earthen surface
as mankind warms himself from the frigid nights
as the fires of the divine
 burn through the frozen skies
sending warmth to man to keep him alive,
supporting his dependence on his lifeline,
his food that keeps him alive,
his spirit that he needs to give him strength,
the voices that tell him to be grateful,
the memento that tells him not to forget
where the fires came from.

They send the warmth to the frozen gardens,
from Winter's curse to Summer's blessing,
that the dead shall rise again,
that the days will be filled with relief and pleasure,
that the Earth is the educator of life
on its rendezvous with the sun,
the one who's suffused in wisdom,
that pleasure is built from the aftermath of pain
and its place in the being,
the place that cries out to be alleviated
from all distress that settled in,
that to know pain is to know pleasure
from the pleasure from its rising above it.

Earth and sky and its marriage to the sun,
the sacred fires from the mouth of the divine,
the goodwill cast about the land,

the eternal charity from the mind of the divine,
the plan carried out through the ages
that never deviates from its course,
the plan for the fires of the divine
to keep burning throughout all time.

Euphonic Winds

Euphonic winds carrying sweet sounds to me
from ambrosial gardens and a sunrise reveille

hymns of the heavens come down to earth
on velvety shoots and diamond's worth

blowing in my ear as the summer winds blow
and angel breath stirring up the heaven's flow

and sweet music flying toward me in rhyme
dipped in exotic spices and rosemary and thyme

melodic birds singing psalms from the upper skies
a symphony of the earth and of the mystic wise

a celestial ride on a rainbow up and back
and a falling from a cloud through a narrow crack

 the oncoming winds of a euphonic origin
in cadence to the pulse of heaven's disclipine,

the marching of the air to the ear of the heart
the sweetening of the skies right from the start

a new vehicle with a poetic mind to steer it
a new language, a new fragrance, a new spirit

and me with my ear to the euphonic winds
and me, dancing with my emancipated limbs
oh such air so sweet, to me thou cometh.

Secret Earth

Earth of deep secrets, her engines beneath,
her lava flows, her deep-seated rage,
her moods waiting to explode at any time,
her pride flowing through her breasts,
her milk saturated with sugar and spice,
her effervescent veins stuffed with salt and riches,
her mother lodes hiding way down deep as
she clamps them down with metal clamps,
living her life of glamour and luxury,
 hoarding everything for her stingy self,
keeping her secrets under lock and key,
her body an enigma only known to her,
her caves leading to another exotic cave,
a land darkened by the shade of diabolic wings,
engines cranking up the evil spirits
with satanic blood running through the cold,

and maternal demeanors,
and rivers of the angels,
saviors out of the fires.
high flying knights in brazen armor,
hands of the daughters of mercy
pushing up all that is good to the surface,
mothers carrying on the deeds of motherhood,
rising up through the skin of her earth,
praising the sun and the God that it is,
drinking in the rain and all that is good,
oh, mother of whimsical moods, mystery,
kindness, goodness, mercy, and beauty,
thou art indeed a capricious woman.

Summer Soup

Residue of the oceans is sitting in the fields.
Stagnation is in the air to what it yields.
Neptunian creatures crawl into the skin
and shed their tears up to a withstanding brim.

  The air became saturated as the ocean's took over
and moved onto the land with a briny odor,
spreading a liquid haze oe'r the quiet meadows
and up into the eyes of the watchful plateaus.

 Blood is on the menu for an August appetite,
a mosquito's paradise in the epicurean twilight.
A sumptuous feast as summer's soup du jour
is the remedy for an empty stomach for a cure.

Hail to the ensuing October breeze
and the shivering of all the winter trees
and the annihilation of the August parasite
as the cold is all that's left to bite.

Chameleon Forest

Chameleon forest of ever-changing colors
from white to green and all the others,
change from cooler nights and shorter days
to blend with the climate as it sways.

Vibrant golden leaves to red and to brown,
 beauty's last stand before they hit the ground,
await the arrival of Winter's whited snow
to blend with the colors as the cold winds blow.

Mystery Road

Along the way before Martin's Winding appears,
a road not taken and by-passed through the years,
is still a mystery to me that makes me wonder.
When I see it again shall I begin to sunder?

My beaten path has my tracks still in the road.
The beeline to my destiny is growing old.
If I take the road a new world will open up,
satisfy my curiosity and get me out of my rut.

Is the new road a part of this or another world?
Does it end or does it twist around and furl?
Is it made of asphalt or of a creatural flesh?
Does it rise from the bottom up to a hill-top crest?

Is it submerged and breathe through aquatic gills?
Does it move and swim around all the hills?
Does it lay flat on the ground or move on its own?
Will it take me where I want to go or let me roam?

Does this new road exist out there for only me?
Does it lay still for others as far as they can see,
or does it move around and twist and turn,
playing with them like to me with no concern?

I shall drive upon it the next time I go.
What can happen for this to me I owe.
I will never know what kind of world is there
until I find out and to others can I share.

Silhouettes

Gallery in the unsettled skies at dusk
in the lap of the humid air,
skyborne giants piling up cumulus clouds
high in the sky to touch the firmament,
flaunting their beauty for the beholder,
silhouetted against the ochred colored sky,
the penumbral faces rolling in the air
with anxiety written on the visible side,
anticipating the rumbling and the
fires of the tempest,

such beauty there is in Mother Nature's gallery,
strobe lights flashing, tempest fires burning,
sending sparks through the nervous clouds,
the clapping of the Thunder Gods
applauding the encore of the quiet that left
and to the turbulence about to begin,
as the clouds sweat and pace and blacken and twist,
silhouetted against the illuminated sky screen,
dusk holding on to her still bright colors,
about to fade with the fading of the penumbra.

Oh-h the pelting rains from the rumbling clouds
silhouetted against the hallowed firmament,
the sweat from the sky engines halfway to heaven,
the remnants from the half divine place in the skies,
the evidence that there is something pure above us,
the pure that started up the engines
that brought the holy rains down upon our soiled lands
to keep us alive and grateful and cleansed.

Secrets in the Trees

Secrets stored inside as the seasons run,
 a silent knowing of the roving sun,
encased in an armor of iron and wood,
in rigid vaults to the weather withstood,

secrets of the rising from low to high,
 the lowest rung up the ladder to the sky,
a phenomenon of nature's handiwork
as seasons call for vigilance on alert,

the bracing for the winter's heavy frost,
when dreams of a fertile green become lost
and the leaves begin to lose their color
as they brood and look to one another,

a mandate from the commanding weather,
a change to one and all together
 from a secret source from deep inside,
a botanical brain implanted as a guide,

a complex river of activity created
by the warmth of a soothing breath awaited
that knows when summer's coming near
to start the flowing through channels clear.

Secrets in the trees are still a mystery
 as the seasons roll on from heaven's decree,
 the lore of the forest ingrained in the wood
and the years gone by as they always should
in strict accordance to the seasonal commandments.

Oh Glorious Curtain

Oh glorious curtain seated
in thy sacred place in the morning sky,
thy majestic opening to the new day,
pulling back to reveal the chameleon clouds
that change color with each of thy movements,
after the blackness that shrouded the night,
to the purple hue of the perforated clouds,
then to the bright yellow upon thy opening,

then sitting back and watching the sun
on its westward journey, a mission of duty,
shining a light upon all that is living,
all that it made to live and all to keep it alive,

oh glorious sun, the giver and keeper of life,
the embodiment of God the creator,
the divinity in the eyes of man,
the oldest engine that keeps on churning,
that stays fixed in its eternal location,
the proof that it couldn't be man-made,
that no mind can be that intelligent,
something from a different sort of man,
maybe a spirit behind the creation of man.

Maybe that spirit is our God of supreme intelligence
and we are to be thankful for all he's done for us
and be thankful for that glorious curtain that
pulls back each morning to reveal the sacred sun
that gives us life and keeps us alive
and all else that lives on this beautiful Earth.

White Velvet Skies

'Neath the blue firmament
that touches the outskirts of heaven,
where the brittle white canopy
that covers up the unstable clouds,
breaks up and drifts apart
like the foam of the sea,
the listless velvet fragments laze about,
drifting, wandering, lolling,
waiting to be pushed along by
the hands of the wind,
flaunting themselves in view of poetic eyes
that gaze at the splender of the sky.

Images of a majestic world come to mind;
rolling rivulets, crystal waters, pure gardens,
savory fruits, cottony landscapes, silky islands,
rhythmic waves, easy drifting, songs of the seagulls,
a world in the eyes of the dreamer coming true.

Stories unfold before him as he gazes upward.
Puffed up silky white gardens roll along the sky.
 Velvet cathedrals drift along with the winds.
Psalms of the saints are voiced in their blowing.
Hymns of the angels echo through the halls.
Music of the heavens melts all restless moods.
The world is calm, peaceful, beautiful,
and oh, so beautiful.

Scarlet Embers

Fires of the dawn and scarlet embers
dancing on the clouds as morning splendors
effervescent skyscapes for poetic eyes
black and scarlet in the higher skies

from fires rising from the earthen rooms
through dark corridors and cryptic tombs
up through the cracks in the punctured ground
and the inconsistent hills scattered all around

 morning galleries coming into view
and scarlet embers and pink clouds too
and trumpets sounding the dawn of the day
playing reveille as the embers fade away

behold a new day as an ever-changing gallery
as the sun stays afloat and then grows weary
and crimson colored skies are all around
as eventide comes to pull it back down

then the journey through the bowels of the earth
running through caves and waterways in mirth
then opening the tombs to go to sleep
until time to rise and to the skies to greet
then the changing again as it ever wanders
to scorch the clouds with scarlet embers

Crocuses of Gallantry

Crocuses of gallantry cutting through the snows,
steadly rise from stouthearted embryos
as heroines braving the cruel winter's wrath,
digging through late Winter's snows to make a path.

They rise up above in their vibrant green crowns
while soon to be donning their elegant purple gowns
to meet the Springtime with the finest of wear,
performing their rites in ceremonious flair.
An ode to the beauty of the early Spring
and to what all the different seasons bring.

Green and Greener

Shades of green run along the verdant,
 touching the sky from an earthly slant.
Fields of corn and fields of barley
wake up and sing with morning's reveille.

They flaunt their vibrant green attire
and the corn keeps growing high and higher.
The barley sways to the rhythm of the wind
like dancers dance and swimmers swim.
Summer's setting is a vivid longing for the eyes
as the beauty of Mother Nature complies.

Runaway Shadows

Runaway shadows begin to
exit at Martin's Winding
as the tall, bulging Elm Trees start to undress
in preparation for Winter's Ball,
running away into the deep abyss.
They strip the road of all its
beauty from the leaves that
cast their animated shadows that
tell a story of the sun's rendezvous
with the Earth Ball that never stops spinning.

They expose the nakedness of the trees
and tune up for the song of Winter,
"A Symphony of the Winds,"
that howl through the branches
and accompany the chattering crows.
They liven up the song of Winter
with a rhythm and melody
and give a pulse of life to Martin's Winding
that doesn't move away with the shadows
but after a while, they climb
out of the abyss
in time for the inundation of Spring.

Hallelujah again!, the time to rejoice,
the time for the Symphony of the Birds,
the time for the earth to rejuvenate,
the time for its heart to start beating again,
and the time to see the shadows
splashing across the road at Martin's Winding.

Autumn Fields

Fields turning orange at harvest time,
pumpkins getting ripe on the hearty vine
as orchards stretch up to the lower skies
in regimental rows so dazzling to the eyes.

Apple trees are ready for the picking
to be eaten soon as time is ticking.
The bounty of life is set for the harvesting
and at the table we ask for God's blessing.

A Provisional Setting

Mother Nature paints the rolling hills,
 the summer greens and winter frills,
the flowery meadows and rising verdants,
and the snow on top as it poses and flaunts.

It dances with the wind without a sound
 and falls at night 'til it lies upon the ground,
 earthbound traveling from skyward born
in time to see the sunrise in the early morn.

It brags about its beauty for only a while
until the rays of the sun start to smile.
They melt her beautiful work of art
as the baren peaks begin to fade to dark.

A frustrated artist is Mother Nature this time,
but she puts her trust in her seasonal design
as winter turns into spring and summer into fall
and provisional settings answer nature's call.

Sky Man

Big man up in the little sky
 at the concordant podium,
waking up from his deep sleep,
hears the cries of the parched earth,
sensing the anxiety of the farmers,
going to work in his celestial studio,
looking out at the order of the environ,
the lazy skies at peace with themselves,
the pacific mood in the face of the firmament,
the empty expression and pastel colors,
the settling in of the indifferent skies
and the deep sleep that they fell into.

Grabbing his paddle and waking up
the sleepy skies,
he stirs them up and disrupts the
flow of the feeble calm.
He riles up the still wind.
He sends the sun deep into the abyss.
He summons the clouds to assemble
and smashes them into each other.

He brings chaos to the lazy mood.
He is a disrupter of the established peace
and the cadence of the quiet skies.
He is a benevolent beast,
angry but kind, tyrannical but heedful,
a beast with charity written on his face,

a rainmaker that dampens the spirit
but revives the withered crops in the field,
 a hero who answers the calls of the needy.
All hail to the Sky Man and his heedful deeds.

Inferno Forest

Human nature and Mother nature,
side by side with two minds and souls,
the good and the evil in a heated battle,
tries to win over in total domination
with pleasure as the diabolic lure
and divinity as the feeble underdog,

Forests, the playground of the beast,
built up with fertile vegetation in mind,
rises up from nature's constructive mind,
 spreading greenery out as a vibrant tablecloth
with fruited trees reaching up to heaven,
cutting through halos and clouds,
basking in the divine nature of the sun
and availing itself for the needs of man
in obedience to the mandates of the divine,

then ravaging them with inferno fires
like a child destroying his own sandcastle,
running with the good and evil in his mind,
letting the devil in to control his actions,
having fun with the consequences,
unaware of the misery inflicted,
an innocent caper turned into a major catastrophe,
a running with no foresight in mind.

Interno fires are born out of the
wildness of the sun
from its careless maintenance of the forest,

its evil side influencing its actions,
the child in it being devilish and imprudent,
its nature too much like human nature,
its drying out the succulent vegetation
and turning it into kindling for the heat of the sun
like children building sandcastles
then destroy them with laughter.

Mother Nature is a child with a supreme power,
of goodness, love, and evil unsurpassed.

Furnaces of Summer

Cool waters in the yards of Neptune
are far, far away from
the searing heat of the sun,
sleeping in the arms of winter's hideaways,
smoothing out the oceanic highways
 for the busy seafarers to sail upon,
rolling with the rhythm of the deep-sea engines,
swaying with the gentle crests and troughs
in cadence to the easy motion of the waves
like the rocking of mother's arms to sleep.

Seafarer's paradise is the taming of the wild waters
under the commands of the cool air authorities
that govern the kaleidoscopic seas
that succumb to a higher authority as the
rays of the sun grow increasingly stronger,
strong enough to ignite the furnaces of summer,
the unleashing of the wildness that lives
in the bowels of the malleable waters
that succumb to the authority of the warmth
as it singes the skin of the underwater beast
asleep in the furnace of the cool waters
that grows angrier as the heat intensifies
until it wakes up from its winter's nap and
rises up to the surfaces in rebellion.

It storms about in a rage that stirs the seas
that ruffles the waters and watches them swirl
and laughs at the ships as they toss and turn.

All hell is broken loose as it rises up
and wreaks havoc as the summer furnaces
run full blast in the searing heat
creating a rhythm in cadence to
the swirling winds above.

Beautiful rhythm of the hurricane winds,
beautiful sight above the skin of the clouds,
beautiful white sea that rides on their backs,
beautiful slow moving circles round and round,
beautiful skyscape that glistens from the upward sun,

Ugly head of the sea beast under the clouds,
ugly smiles from his contorted face,
ugly laughing as he sees what he has done,
ugly rain and spit from his twisted mouth,
ugly winds that speed up more and more
that disrupt the peace of winter's air,
that keeps pounding the seas until
they become exhausted and fall to sleep.
Goodnight you devil's advocate
until the warm air comes again
 and ignites your furnace
and makes you rise again.

Demonic Fires

Primal fires from secret places
ignited from the souls from unholy faces

passion from the wild out into the wild
unleashed from the dark by the demon's child

fires stained with blood and yellow spume
a satanic brew from the devil's room

a will and a plan to annihilate the earth
and the manifestation of that plan from its birth

a fervent feeling in the groin to execute that plan
as a voluntary submission to the devil's demand

an accord with his way of life and malicious desires
to rape the Earth with his erotic, gratifying fires

a glorious sight to see the dancing flames
and acquirement of the marauder as he lay claims

a surge of adrenalin rivers filling up the groin
rivulets into tributaries into oceans to adjoin

a flowing of the sordid waters right from the start
a shaking of the spine and of the heated heart

a nearing of the fires upon reaching the last stand
a charring of Mother Nature over all her land

a victory over the quiet Earth and her green forests
a wiping of the sweaty brow as the spirit rests

and an urge to go back home and reload
and wait to travel again that familiar road
after Mother Earth gets up to rise again.

Glory Rider

Ego dresseed up in satin finery
with a puffed up chest and swollen head
a one man show of musical gallantry
a rhythmic galloping of melodic hooves
glory to the house of glory
rushing to the substitute Gods on high
riding on the backs of rainbows
charging up the electric spine
up the ladder to the arms of beauty
supplying more beauty to the beauty
feeling the texture against the skin
a climb with no hands or feet
a rising with a lofted ego in the mind
making up the wind to sail along
a music solo surpassing all other music

an ego that closes the door to advancement
a superficial end that is the end
a gloating with weakened threads
that hold the end together
as reality breaks through and
rains on the parade of glory.

Deliverance

Man of two men, bestial and chaste
with a barrier down the middle
of his soul,
dividing demonic hideaways
from upright plantations,
dividing infernal soldiers from angelic fighters,
habitants of the dark from the seers of the light,
enemy of the divine from the advocates of the Godly,
marauders of the temples from resolute cathedrals,
lovers of the defiled from the extollers of the pure,
executors of pain from the wholesome of mind,
riders of the virus pollen from the hearty forests,
denizens of Gomorrah from the Holy Garden,
partakers in the orgies from the air of the Kingdom,
separated by an iron door with rusted ancient bolts,
keeping the wicked from the righteous,

the wicked imprisoned on its own turf
with bloody claws in hopes of
clawing its way out,
or looking for an explosive
to ignite and blast
  its way through the barrier,

or for a weakening in the man's stable mind,
a new pleasure to bring to his senses,
a seductress to soften his stone heart,
to surrender to the wiles of her scheming mind

and her tender touch and silky skin
as many have done before and forever will;

a rising up of the wicked and
overpowering of the good,

a story of the deliverance of the wicked
to the threshold of the human spirit
and the downfall of man's moral principles.

Savage Innocence

Mother Nature, beautiful child, Eden's ambience,
of humanity sketched out on the drawing board,
embodiment of innocence and purity,
with verdants stretching out into space,
reaching out into the Holy Garden,
greenery dressed up in priestly robes,
flaunting their emerald jewelry,
crawling up the ladder to the highest mount,

Mother Nature, a lady of solid resolutions,
of no relenting in her determination,
her ways fixed as she was
 in the dawning of light,

commanding the clouds to move about,
to water the parched earth,
to make the seedlings rise and
manifest themselves into grapes,

and Mother Nature of a mind of her own,
a child at play in the delicate skies,
a beast grown out of her evil side,
a tyrant that moves the clouds about,
that defies the resolution of order,
that laughs at the harmony of the skies,
that establishes a new order to come about
and ravage the vineyards that she built up
by drowning them with too much water.

an innocent child with a beast hidden inside,
releasing it on a whim, a capricious moment,
a thrilling escapade, a mischievous rant,
 her savage self that rises from her innocence
and preys upon the goodness that she is.

Like a Goddess she is revered.
Like a mother she is consolable.
Like a father she is an exemplar.
Like a lioness she is feared,
but yet admired for her unrelenting power.

Child of the Hood

Child of teachers of teachers
from generations afore,
teachers with only survival of
the fittest on their sordid minds,
lessons taught and lessons learned,
lessons with no future in mind
but a fast road to prosperity
without a civil plan to achieve it
and waiting for it to come about,

a plan to get it today and not tomorrow,
to get it with no skills or education,
to get it by force and not by acquirement,
to get it by deception and not integrity,
a plan of survival of the fittest,
a lifelong flirtation with life and death,

poor child with the hood in his soul,
of past generations of misguidance,
of friendship with misguided friends,
a comradery that makes him feel wanted
on a journey to an early death,
not able to break the mold
and rise above the mentality.

Poor child of the hood,
we don't need you on our turf.

To the Cellars of Perdition

Falling down to unknown depths
from high homes and pure thoughts
and each day a further falling
with the dark side of man in control,
pushing him down the stairs
of shoddy palaces with chipped paint
amid old gardens that lost their luster,
showing him the pleasures of sin
from the bloody rumpled sheets of Babylon
and the feeling of the conscience draining away
and how it romanticizes a further falling,

the airy feeling of flying through the open earth
and singing above the thunder
and riding on a crackling lightning bolt,
down and down and further down
with the Prince of Darkness at the helm,
laughing at the God in him while they sailed over
 Pleasure's Isle with Gomorrah's wind,

and over dark seas that hide the broken ships
and tombs of the crumbling seamen,
gone forever in Davy Jone's locker
and their ghosts howling above the waves,
an assemblage of friends
 of the dead sea society
pulling at the sleeves
to come and join their group

where conscience used to be
and will never be again,

down, down, down to the cellars of perdition
where the Prince of Darkness reigns.

Death of the Conscience

Conscience with a gag over its mouth, loses more credibility as its influence lessens and its voice becomes fainter in the mind of the man moving toward perdition more so as each day passes by. Its horns become worn out from so much usage. Its frustrations grow stronger from not being heard, but yet it still perseveres as God never gets worn out and subsequently does not give up.

Yet the voices full of strength and wisdom are at full volume, dictating the rules of morality. For his punishment they spread a distaste through his being. Even though the sound is still there, he tries to not let it affect his demeanor. Then the voices are finally silenced as he reaches the state of perdition. When he kills someone, he has no regret for what he did.

To his dismay though, here come the voices again loud and clear as he lies on his death bed. He reflects on his life and regrets the way he lived it. He's scared for what might happen to him when the white wings of death take him away. He is finally intimate with God again as he was when he was drinking his mother's milk. He is reformed now but yet responsible for his killings. He lived his life as a man in hiding, looking over his shoulder for someone seeking revenge. The death of his conscience led the way for the life he lived.

Intrinsic Mandates

Intrinsic mandates from the mind of God,
the rules of discipline of staff and rod,

conscience implanted, the seed of the blessed
in times of turmoil and uncertainty addressed,

a counselor that lives in caves down under
endowed with wisdom and spiritual wonder,

a hidden saint born out of loyalty and sapience,
walled in with no desire to jump over the fence,

who knows what evil lurks on the other side
as he counsels and lets all inquisitors decide,

who implants an uneasy feeling in their heart
when their decision leads them down into the dark,

and a contented feeling for their strict obedience,
their loyalty, faith, introspection, and diligence,

a man without a conscience as a guide through life
 a man living with a contented feeling deprived,

or a contented feeling begotten from the evil done,
the worst of all on this side of the sun,

a beast inside a man with his conscience abandoned,
 siding with the devil to his authority succumbed.

Man with his conscience weighing heavily in his soul
is a man the world needs to lead and take control.

Upward Pilgrimage

As if the soil down under was a warm cathedral
 on a journey to a downward pinnacle
where the voice of God reached the seed
and told it to rise up and follow his lead
up through the soil and into the summer's air,
the leaf stalk rises as it climbs each stair.

It peaks its head out to where it laid claim
and spreads its leaves to the sun and rain
as it woships its God who gave it strength
for its pilgrimage from the roots so entrenched.

Religionless

The poor man with no religion,
with nobody to tell him who his enemy is,
or what label to be classified under,
or what despotic leader there is to punish him
for disobeying his man-made mandates,
and to burn in hell for making his own decisions,

the poor man with no religion,
 with only just a love in his heart for God
and a strict adherence to his own conscience,
his innate dividing line between good and evil,
following the commandments directly from God,
his charity and good will ingrained,
his religion whose doors are open
in his soul from dawn to dawn
and not only on Sunday Mornings,

the poor man with no religion;
no Methodism, no Hinduism, no Catholicism,
no Islam, or no Presbyterianism in him.
He must be lost with no label attached to him.
He must not know that he has to have one to love.
He has to open the windows to his soul
only when his religion says he can
and he has to be prepared
to battle all other religions' doctrines.

Or he can just remain being himself,
loving God and obeying his conscience

that comes directly from God and not
filtered through different religions
that are all at odds with each other.

Love is the consecration of all religion
and the ladder to keep climbing
to be intimate with God in his Holy Kingdom.

Muscles

Big mountains, tempest fury,
big mouth, power empowering,
pounding flesh, uprooting trees,
black sun rising, dusty rain,
flocks of geese out of cadence,
rogue waves in random bursts,
virgins begotten and thrown away,
hell flying to the upward skies,

muscles running through the brain
armed with spears and battle-axes,
flaunting their power and strength,
dressed up in their shiny armor
with razor spikes on the feet,
riding on steeds with heavy hooves,
pounding the delicate clouds,
cursing at the way of the winds,
calling the natural elements their own,
putting the stars in their pockets,
stripping the universe with their greed,
shaking up the skies with their big mouths
until their final ride into the blackened sunset,
struck down by a mightier power,

and the white wings of death claim their bodies
and the meek wait until old age to die.

Future's Destiny

The plan for us to obey
is prescribed at the time of creation,
sunken deep into the soul of man;
laborer, technicion, or artist,
that will lead him upon his earthly mission,
shedding a light on the road to follow
in order to accomplish it,
endowing him with a certain gift
that makes it easier to travel upon.

It is administered from divine sources.
It cannot be a scapegoat that we make
responsible for our crimes.
It is given to us to maintain morality
by obeying its mandates
 to keep the earth alive and safe
as long as possible.

Why should our creator destroy something
that was within his plan to make it eternal?

The Pumping

Engine in my bike and engine in the glands
adrenalin pumping into mortal wonderlands

and the crowds cheering as I mount up to ride
my guts all knotted up and churning inside

snaky road up ahead and Grim Reaper waiting
when I round the first bend with my inside shaking

sweet smell of liquid dynamite fills my nostrils
in gilded gardens of death with all the frills

rivers bending their banks with their heavy power
their persistent pounding every minute every hour

running into my spirit as I look at the road ahead
staying with me until I finish alive or dead

racing with me as I race around the devil's course
infernal curves, snaky turns, transcendent force

the power of death matched up with my mortal spirit
my insides grinding and pushing bit by bit

my internal engine at the speed of my bike
up to the max and then out of sight

angel of death with me around the first turn
taking me home as I crash and burn

my pumping abated and my pace slowing down
my last breath breathed with heaven all around

my racing up into the sky is my final race
with all the other racers resting in God's grace

Fast and Faster

Full speed ahead, feeling the adrenalin
surging through the veins,
bulldozing its way to the heart,
bringing sweet smelling roses
and barrels of caffeine and spices
 to galvanize the spirit,

sending the blood to flood the chambers,
sending it over the highest cliffs,
massaging the spine with iron feathers,
riding on crazed gazelles
faster that the lightning that hits the ground
feeling their hooves kicking the skin,

flying with the birds and Pegasi
into the wilds and back out again
into the heart of the insane,
feeling the glory of life and its derangement,
how it invades the order of reason,
the rules of life in disarray;
not with the prevention of death in mind,
but death and its glorious welcoming
through its open gates,
paralyzing the mind from the consequences,

fast and faster, full speed ahead
with the adrenalin pumping into the spirit
with life and death at the controls
and the sweet feeling of its surge

fueling the heart with more power
and numbing the mind to reason
as the ability to stop becomes less and lesser
until the adrenalin carries you
all the way into the Valley of Death.

Broadcast Blues Man

Herbert the broadcast blues man of fame,
lives in his house on Cherry Lane,
too scared to come out of his rubber room
in fear of the world caving in too soon.

A victim of too much TV he is for sure,
for him he thinks there is no cure.
There's no place to go when the bombs go off,
when the world blows up and sends him aloft.

 Herbert, too scared to come out and breathe,
glued to the news, can't get up and leave.
The bombs are coming, the guns are blazing,
Everybody's nuts and the world's gone crazy.
"Live a little Herbert and go outside.
Have some fun and enjoy the ride."

Evacuation of the Nymphs

In the density of summers' forests
where forest nymphs frolicked and danced
behind the copious leaves
that covered up their nakedness,
nocturnal Autumn arrived on schedule
to steal their abounding floral shields
that they danced behind.

The teeth of the frost bit into
the trees that supplied their cover up
and the cold chased them
away into oblivion.

Some say they went to the southern climes.
Some say they became invisible and
whistled like the wind through the barren trees.
Some say they will never come back again.
Some say they appealed to the authorities
to loosen the grip of Winter tide to
bring back the warmth so they
can frolic and dance again.
Some say they armed themselves
with spears and battle axes and
fought like hell to bring their shields
back so they can hide behind them again.

They are gone. (never to return?)
Now I can only see the empty spots
left behind where they used to be.

Even though I couldn't see them
last summer, I can
 imagine them frolicking
behind the leaves.
Please come back again
Nymphs of the forest green.

Song of the Angels

Harps of soft velvet and cushioned melodies
of scarlet sunrises and ambrosial reveilles

a soft stroking with fingers dipped in honey
the proper ingredients in a euphonic recipe

of beauty and its embodiment in poetic rhyme
a smooth riding on clouds sublime

a probe into deep fields and to the beyond
echos of harmonic tones to the maestro's baton

melodic tears falling upon sympathetic strings
 lullabies in rhythm as heaven sings

tapping of the rains in a hypnotic pulse
dancing round and round to a swirling waltz

heaven's language floating in the melodic air
a sacred pilgrimage to an earnest prayer

song so sweet and song so hallowed
purifying the air as the melodies flow

falling through space and riding up the spine
climbing into the heart in a timeless time

a song on a mission to soothe the spirit
that relaxes the anxiety bit by bit

oh sweet music of therapeutic mysteries
nursing the soul as the wizard oversees

as the angels play on their magic harps
and the music flows in to flood the hearts

Pacific Dust

From the pacific skies comes the falling dust
in the mystic winds from an outward thrust,
from a bursting star in the night-time sky,
rocks catch on fire, break loose, and liquify.

Lava cools down and splits into pieces
and pieces turn back into dust and freezes
and falls through the sky to planet earth,
the land of madness since the time of birth.

The dust falls upon everyone everywhere,
lovers of war and hatred in the air,
seeping down into their restless soul,
moving into their spirit and taking hold.

At last the whole world is at peace;
No more armies and no more police.
There is magic in the skies up above
with all the madness turned to love.

The only way it can be done
is by wizards with their magic spun,
showering the earth with pacific dust.
Oh such dreamers that we dreamers are.

Melodious Tears

Melodious tears drawn from melancholy wells
symphonic rivulets flowing out of eye born swells

music pistons pumping melodies into the heart
dipped in honey and drifting through the dark

into a mystical, thick maze where passion is born
where music and tears and love all take form

and the stirring causes a mysterious uprising
a peaceful subduction, a wondrous hypnotizing

and passion becomes a river in a gentle flowing
and gaining speed with the intensity growing

and the tears and the melody all mingle together
drifting through the air as light as a feather

and falling like raindrops upon our eager ears
and into canals as the cluttered mist disappears

and the players play on with tears in their eyes
pumping melodies inside to make our spirits rise

and the new rains become tears falling down
into our parched fields of black and brown

and the risen spirits take us into fields of bliss
and sink into us like a mother's tender kiss

and our new paradise is full of beauty and warmth
and as easy as in a still summer's morn

oh, music so sublime, so teary, so passion filled,
so tranquillizing, so calm with peace instilled
with a melody to send you upward on high
so you can sprout your wings and fly and fly.

Hands in the Music

Hands so soft and woven into silk
with sweet succulence and mother's milk
and quiet rivulets in the still of the day
as the zephyrs roam and the breezes sway

and hands as powerful as the rolling seas
with superior strength like the proud oak trees
reaching into the heart with the sound of music
slicing through the walls with teeth and grit

commanding the spirit to break free and dance
into the melodic air with a strange exuberance
sending earthly thoughts into a bewildering maze
and reveling with the sound as the spirit obeys.

Hands in the music are unseen but seen
and all the empty spaces become a dream,
and all the dreams become a melange of sorcery
and sorcery transforms the emptiness into melody.

To the power of music all succumb to its strength
and lets the hands push you up to its very length.

Of Chordal Blending

Of chordal blending and potent saccharine
 and jasmine strewing into music fields therein
 heaven sinking down into earthen plains
 into melodious gardens as harmonic rains

 earth and sky mingling with each other
 harmony lifting the clouds as they hover
 symphonic skies reach into the human heart
 through tender corridors to leave a mark

 certain chords of a certain kind in the blending
 massaging the heart to the spirit ascending
 to certain ears of needs and desires
 to reach down deep and stoke the fires

 melody and harmony, a perfect marriage
 each needing each other to engage
 an inborn mystery of the poetic kind
 the power of music to seek and find

 chordal blending, a touching of the senses
 a magic potion that tears down fences
 a power that sends all dancers dancing
 and others unmoved and only glancing
 then are we who fly on harmonic wings
 up and up to hear heaven as it sings.

The Touch of Melody

Feathers stroking the spirit within,
running to the heart in poetic sin,
stirring up the heart with a wizard's brew,
with old remedies and something new,

softly as is in the early morning haze
and effective as in a fire's blaze,
stirring up moods and shifting them around,
heated dancing with spirits tightly wound,

a casual assembly of flimsy music notes
and the stormy path as the raging river flows,
a melody that digs into the enchanted heart
or the easy drifting of a sky bound lark,

songs of the birds as the authors of music
running through the stirring melodies so quick,
oblivious to the beauty of what they sang,
a simple art of which they laid claim,

an art that ruled the human spirit through
and gave him a potent force to submit to,
a sound, a dance, and another feeling
as the music grows on up to the ceiling
and the dancer dances to that poetic force,
an ode to that music and its melodious source.

Melodic Stories

Stories alone cry for attention,
to bring in someone from out in the cold,
to soften his anxiety and warm his heart,
to fill him up with joy,
wonderment, and knowledge,
to put him in the story as if he
were interacting with the characters
and feeling what they feel.

But words alone depend upon his mental
curiosity to bring him in
but not his automatic response.

Music has its melodic arms to pull him in
and put him in the story,
to feel its moods and transpirations,
to feel it beating in his heart,
to enliven his spirit that comes alive
at the sound of music,
that magic wand that brings the story to him
and places it in his intellect and spirit,
opening the door to his comprehension.

Oh, the power of music,
the velvet arms that bring the story to him,
that forces its way into his callous heart,
that makes him think like the story does,
that makes him feel its many moods,
that takes him to the same places,

over the rough terrain, the stormy seas,
the azure skies, the fruited plains,
breath-taking sunrises and sunsets
that boatswains and helmsmen see every day,
or into the arms of a beautiful woman,
or into the mind of a poet, a musician,
a sage, a priest, a holy man,
or a madman, a thief, or a killer
and their temperaments and desires
that only words alone can't describe
but portrayed by the sound of music
that brings him into the story.
Oh, sweet music and thy power of persuasion.

Wind & Melody

Silent song, the air with no obstruction,
nothing to bend it, to shape it, to embellish it,
to color it, to make it sing,
a river without a bank, without a name,
a story without a plot, a poem without a tear,
a harp with no strings, a trumpet with no valves,
  air left alone with no guide to steer it,
pleading for a something to run up against,
a wall, an opponent, a raging river in between,
an embodied angel to impede its wayward running
and pass it on to another obstruction
 to anoint it, bend it, give it another color,
another pitch, another language, another volume,
breathing more life into it to keep it going,

air into wind into tunnels into obstacles,
into gilded walls, into heavenly pistons,
cranking out psalms to the glory of music,
chanting canticles inside hidden cathedrals,
consecrating the new air outside the tunnel,
out of the bell of the hallowed trumpet,

wind & melody, a heavenly mixture,
a conversion of air into a sound of beauty,
a passing through sacred obstacles to get there,
but the air that needs a wind
that needs a hurdle to pass over
for its melodic shaping
so to land in a paradise of sound.

Prelude to the Power

Easy quiet waters in their lazy silence
their glassy faces and proud elegance

with power in mind but power graduated
a glorious ride and a new pathway created

as a song composed on the way up to the wild
a foundation of golden bricks in melodious style

yet still moving in harmonic ecstasy and quietude
with dreams of power but with turbulence subdued

lovely climb with utmost devotion to every step
sensitive with a tender touch as the angels wept

quiet melodies loading up from their arsenals
building up their strength to jump over walls

with harmonic spears dipped in honey and spice
and blazing torches to thaw the ice

riding on a melodious drone and loving each moment
letting the sound fill up the chasms in a glorious ascent

a prelude to the power and a prelude to ecstatic highs
with euphonic climbing and a madness in their sights

a riding on a lightning bolt with a blast of fire juice
to a landing in the power with all hell breaking loose

as the music explodes and paints the clouds black
and what is heard is the lightning bolts crack

and the rockers rock on with the power of sound
from a quiet prelude to a frenzy tightly wound

but a beautiful prelude with beauty to guide
to ignite the fuse that sends power on a ride
lovely melody beautiful power

Melodic Colors

Of thoughts traveling from a secret hideaway
from deep within to the skies on display,
then back down through the rainbow dust,
collecting colors from an outward thrust,

colors come dressed in their noonday attire
of rainbow residue and clouds on fire,
fueling the heart of the man with the horn,
and warming his blood as the melodies form.

Melodies shoot out into the poetic air
soaked in rainbow tears with balladic flair
on stallions galloping with the easy winds
 to the edge of night as the song begins,

to the chameleon sun and its westward setting,
marriage of the day and the night begetting,
of colors inherited from the chasms of love
and the wind and the rain and the sky up above.

 Beauty enters the music with its silky fingers
and settles in its soul as the sweetness lingers
for a minute or an hour from an eternal wish,
staying for a time or a moment too brisk.

Oh sweet melody of colors in thy warming
that cling to the spirit from rainbows forming,
stay with me and guide my steps
as I travel down to its quixotic depths;
oh such sweet music as thou art.

Music Power

Music power, beacons in the dark,
narrator of the universe,
portrayers of certain epochs,
storytellers in the melodic air,
founders of universal alliance,
tranquilizer of the hostile,
mobilizers of the immobile,
dethroners of the emperors,
empowering forces of the weak,
building iron hearts to put inside them,
leading them to the threshold of their dreams,

simple notes drifting through the listless air,
falling upon the sand and shedding their colors,
violets showing their might,
dancing with the marauding hurricanes,
fragility showing its hidden
strength, climbing jagged cliffs,
taming the beasts of the wild,
curling up with them at bedtime,

power unleased and power subdued,
power sweetened by the sweetest wines,
power anointed by the wand of the high priest
power drenched by the tears of the virgin,
power put to bed by a mother's lullaby,
power softened by its mother's tears,

power moistened by the dews of heaven,
dressed up in the colors of a rainbow,
melting into the radiance of it,
 falling upon the ashen graves,
seeping through the ground
to the catacombs below,
breathing life into everyone and everything,
telling all to rise and dance to the music,
and dance and dance and dance to the power.

String Team

Orchestral string players, devoted to precision,
placing it in high regard,
lovers of teamwork, fraternal harmony,
one music family undivided,
 each supported by the other,
egos subdued and blended into one
 with one goal in mind,
 to make one proud sound,
 one solid reinforcement
from one family working together
building a segment that the music needs,

taking in the music as it comes their way,
loving every note with a whole heart,
reaching into its tender heart with tender ears,
hearing it breathe, hearing it sing,
sensitizing themselves to its sensitivity,
devoting themselves to the love
that pours out in the music,
the God given sound that music is
with a desire to become part of it,
to enhance it by blending into it,
to glorify themselves by being united with it,
by placing themselves on the same echelon
that the music rides upon,

up to the High Holy Kingdom
that the music reaches up to,
riding with it as it starts its ascension with

the pride of being a member of the string team,
the basses, cellos, violas, the violins,
the team that works together as one unit,
all playing in meticulous unison
as if they were the planets
in total accord for an eternity.

Song of the Pipes

The song of the bagpipes cuts through the air,
 over the moors and hills with an Irish flair,
songs of the battles and songs of romance,
songs that make me get up and dance.

How can I deny that music does things to me,
how it lifts me up and sets me free,
how the pipes resonate through my being
as I think of my Sweet Molly in the early Spring?

Painter's Undertaking

Thoughts presented and promises undertaken
the search for beauty and more again

 visions forming and running through the mind
captured and admired and fervently enshrined

a faithful oath so ingrained in the heart and soul
to stay on beauty's path in complete control

to envision the canvas as a painting complete
with colors and shapes and rapture sweet

to work he commits himself with God as a guide
 stroking his brush with a new feeling inside

creating a Shangrila with such beauty abound
inviting him in to come and look all around

to marvel at his work and praise himself
from his lowly place to his upper shelf

and invite the crowd to come inside and see
come into his world to set their spirits free

painting complete and new world come upon
a raising of the esteem to an upper echelon.

The undertaking did what it set out to do;
to bring a new exhilarating world into view.

The Sanctioning

Let it all hang out.
Release your aggression.

War has been declared.
Free the beast that lives deep inside.
Make yourself feel better in the soul.
You have the ruling class's permission.

Go with the flow of the energetic
force within your system.
Feel the adrenalin surging
through your being.

Tear down the cities and buildings.
Violate the enemys' precious virgins.
Forget about the ethics ingrained in you.

Relive your childhood and
gloat over what you have done.
Smash your toys against the wall.
Pull your dog's tail and make him yelp.
Give yourself an excuse for your evil deeds.

The time has finally come
to act according to the influence
that the evil has within you
and the evil ruling class that
sanctioned you to act in that way.

Let it all hang out, little macho man.

The Girding

Mother Nature in the throes of the wild,
That beast kicking up the quiet seas,
Defying the rules of civility and inhibition,
Her love affair with passion and the lust,
Her letting down of her silky locks,
Her flirting and smiling at the devil,
Her children unguarded, unprotected,
Standing in the line of sight of the beast,
That nice man with a hidden nefarious side,
That knows no line between age and reason,
Or innocence and maturity,
Or willingness and reluctance,
That lets his passion rule his world,
His covenant with the wildness of nature,
His throwing himself in the midst of it
With his loins on fire and lust in his heart,
The bestial side of his two sided self,
His animal passion that takes over,
His natural self in the world of pleasure,
His embracing the begotten feeling,
His losing of his self in rapture,
In the throes of nature in her wilderness,

The girding of that natural feeling,
The God self speaking inside his mind
With reason rising to the height of passion,
The shifting of reason to the senses,
The listening to her vulnerability,
Her untainted loins exposed

To the fury of love, her steamy limbs,
Her nervous smile, her childish pleas,
Her innocence written on the face of love,
His passion sinking like a wounded ship,
His fatherly influence taking over,
The contentment of God within,
The pleasure of paradise thwarted,
For the taming of the wild beast
Called "Human Nature."

Thank God for sensibility, conscience,
Reasoning, compassion, and the
Girding at the height of passion.

House on Vulture's Hill

The haunted house up on Vulture's Hill,
the site of the McFarland family kill,
when two men fought over a poker game,
drew their guns and then took aim.
They fired their guns 'til one of them dropped.
Then the loser shot his family and wouldn't stop.

McGregor the culprit, ran away ne'er to come back
and the trees turned gray and the sky turned black.
The robins flew away and the vultures came to roost,
feasting on the rotted bodies as all hell broke loose.
The only sound came from the voices in the wind,
the voices of the dead torturing him for his sin.

"Come back you bastard and pay for what you did.
You can't go free in the places that you hid.
We know where you are so why don't you come out?
We have a score to settle and there's no doubt."

'Twas the only sound heard from up on Vulture's Hill,
the eerie sounds from the voices in a shrill,
where the dead wouldn't stay dead
until McGregor came to justice climbing up ahead;
so the vultures will have another body on their land,
the culprit who murdered the Mc Farland band.

He scaled the hill and climbed up to his fate
as the dead met him at the rusty old gate.

With their axes ready to chop off his head
 they swung at him until he fell and lay dead.

After the vultures ate, they all flew away
and the trees began to lose their gray.
And the green leaves came back to root,
and came alive as the sky turned blue.
Then the eerie voices all faded away
as the gentle breeze made the branches sway.

Then Vulture's Hill took on another name;
Emerald Hill as the killing came to fame.

Castle Hill

On a hill where the trees have no life
and the bands of the dead with drums and fife,
play on at the gates of the olden castle
where Dracula and his evil spirits dwell.

Those who ventured up the craggy hill
made it to the castle in time for the kill,
ne'er to come back to say where they went
as all hell broke loose and released its scent,
and the witches and the bats swirled around
the Autum moon to never touch the ground.

History of a Rock

Atop of Kingly Mountain, away from civilization there is a rock, an insignificant hinderance you will find while walking along the way, but its historic value is extremely significant and compelling. How did it get there? Was it formed when the spirit moved across the waters? Did it reposition itself when the mountains were being formed? Did the ancestors of Adam see it? Did early man use it for a weapon or a tool? Did it become repositioned during the Ice Age? Did it keep its form? Did the seasons mottle it? Is it a fragment of a bigger rock? Was it ever submerged in water? This is a mystery that no one could ever know.
If eternal man sat by and watched it, he could tell you, but since he is mortal, he can't. If there were records kept and handed down through generations, we would know. But since the one rock is so insignificant, there wouldn't be any records. There is only one person that knows the answer; the man who created the stone, and he is not a man but a spirit. If you don't believe in the spirit, you probably don't care. If you believe in it, you can find the spirit within you to marvel over the wonderment and history of every rock that was ever created. Thanks be to God.

Tommy Boy

Tommy Boy out there with the wolves
amid the battle fields and horses' hooves,
bloody banners and razor teeth,
volcanic breath and hell fire neath,

prancing stallions about the dusty air,
spears affixed and banners flair
where warriors encounter warriors
and the blood spills upon the tainted floors,

lines of steel out there to break on through,
linemen with iron spikes and witch's brew,
rising up from the tombs to take you down
and away ye shall go to be never found.

Football's a nasty business for a lad such as you,
alone in the wilderness agin a savage crew
with fire and guts in their metal veins,
pumping out venom into sinewy chains.

You gave your all and then some more.
You ran with the glory right down to the core.
You searched yourself for your forgotten ire
and breathed some fire into their secret fire.

You done it when all was said and done.
You slayed the beast and beat the drum.
Victory is there for boys like you;
for boys into men into strength come anew.

Tommy Man go out and win some more.
Fight like hell and run up the score.
There's a fire burning and burning bright.
Run and run through the glorious night
and keep winning with your new found self
with fire in the nostrils and victory in thy smell.

Slider in the Nineties

Batter up to the plate he comes to bat,
chewing tobacco as to the ground he spat,
staring at the pitcher with intrepid eyes
 his confidence moved up and up on the rise.

Strike one on the outside corner of the plate.
Strike two outside he swung and took the bait.
Ball one outside but he didn't go fishing.
He looked for the middle of the plate while wishing.

Then he crowded the plate for an outside pitch
and stared down the pitcher that son-of-a-bitch.
He looked for a big fat ball on the ouside corner
to drive it to the opposite field getting warmer.

That slider came at his head in the high nineties,
headed for the outside he thinks he sees

He didn't get out of the way and lost his helmet.
It didn't break and to his temple it struck.
He went down with his hands to his face
and the blood squirted out from that same place.

He laid on the ground and didn't move an inch.
To the hospital he went from where he'd bin.
No more sliders could he ever see again.
They don't play baseball up in heaven.

The Games of Autumn

The leaves begin to fall off the trees
and the temperature drops a few degrees.
The gridiron is cleared for the game to begin
and the cheering starts for the home team to win.

From the opening kick-off until the last touchdown
the ball changed possesion as it flew all around.
But in the end our team went ahead and won.
Congratulations to them when the day was done.

Forsythian Trumpets

Forsythian trumpets heralding in the new spring,
sounding reveille as the meadows sing
songs of revelry to the cold cold earth,
chase away the frost with joy and mirth.

The forsythia blooms to beautify the ground
and the robins are to be once again found
and Mother Nature becomes alive again
and in her traveling through forest and glen.
 The earth rises up to the sounding trumpets
and the earth blends in with the colorful sunsets.
An ode to the inundation of her glorious flowers.

Amazing Thou So Art

Amazing thou so art with thy assuring grace,
thy words of mercy written upon your face,
thy enemy that I am surrenders to your look.
Your pentrating eyes captured me by thy crook.

My road ahead is paved with thy credent hand,
covering up my footprints I left in the sand.
My past was my prison that I chose it to be
until you came with thy grace and set me free.

'Tis I that was blinded by my lifeless life,
my unholy deeds and my everlasting strife.
My faithless journey was my only road ahead
until you rescued me from my life of dread.

Now I am free to praise and call your name,
broken away from my life of wretched shame.
You are my God and my faith to lead me on
in times of now and times beyond.

When you come to take me to your home,
I have no fear of being left alone,
for I'll always have you as my confidant,
my God, my savior, 'tis all that I want.
From thy grace I need nothing else.
Amazing thou so art my God, my God.

Heralds of the Tulips

"Hear ye, hear ye, beholders of the Tulips.
After Winter's wrath come Spring-time benefits.
The gardens are all aglow in yellow splendor
and red and orange of primordial tender.

 Mother Nature is kind to us once again
with her floral decorations and colors' blend
as she flaunts her beauty before our eyes
and tells the Tulips it is time to rise.
Hear ye, hear ye, nature lovers and all."

At the Table

We gather up each and every family member
to come home when comes November.
Just like it was when we were young;
we gather at the table for dinner and fun.

Thanksgiving Day is the day to come together,
from far away places and lands wherever.
Each family member is still in each other's heart,
never to move away and forever stay apart.

Kaleidoscope

Shifting, drifting, colors and shapes
my truths, my prose, my charming scapes

my run-a-way shadows on solid ground
rising and drifting as to heavenly bound

dressed in rainbow colors and harlequin suits
playing on a lazy cloud on dreamy flutes

rising with the upper air and falling with the rain
suspended above all and to where cherubims lain

drinking in the helium and the heavy waters
dancing with the truth and deceptive daughters

calling aeroplanes in the name of iron birds
throwing the real away with abstract words

finding new homes for the firmly entrenched
tightening them up with a quixotic wrench

shifting colors in the maze of the kaleidoscope
my life of ups and downs and persistent hope

of the abstract staying within its rigid confines
and my telling of a story as my spirit shines

Death Before Death

Death of the spirit in defiance of God's will in us,
plants the fear of the unknown of life after death,
the downward spiral of the lust for life,
the helplessness of losing control
over something we can't control,
losing our self-reliance inside,
the strength within us that
prides us on to never give up
as the pistons start running out of steam
leading to the
lethargy of the engines that pump the spirit,
bringing on the resignation of life before death.

The losing of the will to fight
the precursor to death
while waiting for the Grim Reaper
to inject the venom inside is in defiance
of God's will that urges us on to fight the battle,
telling us to focus on the good within us
and not let the future dampen our spirits.

Death is a stepping stone on
the pathway to immortality,
the freeing of the breath from its restless tides
that it will rise and expand and find
God, the master of our lives
who preached to us in our spirit
to seek the secret of death through
the heart of life and bring the mystery

into us and let it unfold
through the spirit in us.

"So, lift your heads high and
long to see the mystery of the
afterlife unfold before you, my friends.
Please do not die before you die."

Artisans of the Arctic

Artisans of the Arctic, working around the clock,
looking for supplies and taking stock,
search for one colossal piece of material
to test its buoyancy and put on trial.

They cut symmetrical pieces of patterned snow,
space them apart then let them go
as a myriad of flakes to ride with the wind
and reach the ground for winter to begin.

Familiarity

A musical performance can't be judged by familiarity alone. If it sounds different, it doesn't mean that it is inferior. It should be judged by skill and the quality of sound. If it is judged by a sound that is familiar only, it can't be a true evaluation. The quality of sound has nothing to do with public opinion. Skill should be what is judged and not familiarity.

As inclination changes, the unstable tide of public judgment changes with it. The quality of sound is not firmly entrenched in the convictions of man and is vulnerable to how the masses think of it. Popular opinion will always be the judge as the followers keep following it and think that it is a true evaluation. And since it seems to be so convincing, it will always be the commanding voice.

Militant Island

In my hours of deep sleep last night, my dreams sped toward me like a vivid saga that stormed into my being and kicked into my divine faith.

There were two Gods, the familiar one of the spirit that oversees the desires of man but sits back and lets the drama of life unfold. Then there was the physical God who oversees all human desires but polices their actions and brings them to justice.

In my dream there was a physical colossal omnipotence up high in the sky also with eyes to see inside the desires of all humanity on earth. They had billions of arms that could reach down and grab all the militants and then drop them off at Militant Island, far away from all who only desire peace and happiness. If the militants want to keep on fighting, so be it. Maybe they can kill each other off, then the problem of the World would be solved.

I know this solution is far-fetched, but it was my dream last night. In reality there is no solution, no Utopia, no justice, and no island big enough to house all the militants. There is just the disregard of the Divine Spirit within that preaches the manifestation of love by only urging humanity to follow the rules and not reprimanding them for their disobedience. There could be no Militant Island in reality. (too bad!!)

The Road to Paradise

The road to paradise is paved with barb that stings the flesh along the way but leads to the highest joy. It proves that wisdom is in the knowing of how pain feels and how much more paradise feels because of it. A joyful man can't truly feel the joy until he has felt the sting along the way.

No one wishes for pain to come, but its natural occurrence plants the seed of hope in his spirit, sending him upon the road to paradise. When he gets there, the true feeling of joy comes naturally, leaving him a joyful man. The deeper that pain carves into our beings leaves more room for joy to fill it back up.

A life without any sorrow and suffering is only a life half lived. A wholesome life is a mixture of pain and sorrow; of sorrow traveling along the road to paradise and finding it at the very end.

The Poor Superstar

We all should feel sorry for the poor superstar quarterback. He didn't have enough money in his bank account to pay the Hooter Girl hostesses that would work in his fifteen million dollar Bell 525 Relentless Helicopter that lands on the deck of his yacht. The poor guy has to pay for only a staff of a few common workers. The Hooter Girls are too expensive. Now he has to suffer though his meal of filet mignon and drink his martinis with nothing to look at while flying through the air.

There should be a charity event that will help him raise enough money to pay the Hooter Girls. If he has nothing to look at, he will be very depressed. We don't want him to feel that way. So if the people would just open their wallets and put $100.00 in the cup, that will make him very happy. No matter how poor you are, if you can't afford a hundred dollars, you should be ashamed of yourself. Can't you feel sorry for someone in such dire need? Don't you want to make someone happy?

Befuddlement Machines

"Hello. You have reached the office of Yuk Yuk Medical Supplies. Please listen to the following options. If you called in regard to a hydraulic slide softener, please press 1. If you wish to make multiple hydraulic slide softener orders, press 2. If you wish one of the items was a different color, press 3. If you like the color but not its shade, press 2 and then 3 again. If that color clashes with the previous color, press 4. Then press 5 if you want it changed. Then press 2 at the same time to cancel out number 3. If you want to cancel out the one you chose, press 6. If number 2 clashes with number 5, press 7. If you follow these simple instructions, your order will be on its way to you right away." said the befuddlement machine.

"But I just called to speak to my friend Leo down there. Can I speak to him or anyone else?" asked the befuddled caller.

"Hello," said the machine, "You have reached the office of Yuk Yuk Medical Supplies. Please listen to the following options. If you called in regard to - - - - " (yadi yada and some more of that same yadi yada again, the whole shmear again, that friggin bull crap again, over and over that $(%@(%!) !"

"What happened to all the people down there at Yuk Yuk Medical Supplies? Did they fade away?" thought he. "Did that befuddlement machine put the hex on them? Did it send them flying up through space or something? I'm going down there and throw that friggin thing in the lake, that &($%^@!^&$ thing !"

And so he went down there and threw it in the lake, and all the people came back to work again.

The Introspection

Your heart knows in silence the secrets of the boundless knowledge within you. Your mind thirsts to tap into the spacious seas that contain all thought and deeds of your past, your triviality that grew into streams that grew into rivers. It calls for you to introspect and find them and use them to build up your self-esteem and direct your course to the shores of your dreams.

True poets can't be molded by the minds of popular appeal. His intrinsic worth is his ability to think for himself and follow what his heart says. If the ideas in his mind elaborated upon the ideas of popular opinion, he will be neglecting what is inside of him, his own accumulated knowledge. His subconsciousness has become his consciousness from his introspection without any outside influence or opinions.

He is a replica of God's creation with the capability of moving culture up to a new echelon. He is the forerunner of what it has become. Popularity breeds more popularity while originality breeds and nurtures culture. Thinkers like him keep it vibrant and flowing and are the cause for its advancement.

Upon Offending Zombies

If you see a Zombie walking toward you down the sidewalk, you shouldn't say, "Hey you Zombie, you piece of crap." That is very offensive. After all, he she or it is a human being with feelings just like you have. Actually, I can't say human being, but it might have been at some time before. Just because it is a member of the minority race, it is just like you and me with a few minor adjustments.

Upon addressing a Zombie in the proper way, you could say, "Top of the morning to you, ole Chap. You sure look quite dapper with that matching set of eye sockets in your head. You don't even need eyeballs in them. You look quite handsome without them," or, "Your skin is the same color of the dashing gray sport jacket I bought yesterday, and that black funk junk that you got oozing out of your scalp is the same color as the beautiful silk tie that I bought to go along with the jacket.

If the Zombie is too far gone, it might be too hard to identify its gender. You shouldn't call it an it. You should refer to it as a sir or ma'am with the utmost respect; something like Sir Zombie, Madam Zombie, or Friend Zombie, though not close enough of a friend to invite to dinner. He or she might smell too bad and ruin the appetite, and besides that, you might be its main course for dinner. When you get to know a Zombie, it has the same characteristics as you and me except it doesn't sleep too much. It just wanders around the streets looking for a friend like you and me. I don't know what it would do if it found a friend. Maybe it is a naughty Zombie. Maybe you shouldn't try to shake hands with it or hug it. If it is naughty, it might have come from an abusive family. Maybe its daddy was a no good for nothing drunken Zombie who gets plastered and kicks the crap out of his boy. They also wander around the streets. You can't try to kick the crap out of the poor boy, because he can't help his nastiness. He might also tell his father, then his daddy will come and kick the crap out of you. They are all just misguided in life. You should feel sorry for them and show them some respect.

So, when walking down the street you should say, "Good day your most handsome, intelligent human being Zombie person." Show some respect to our American citizens and don't be offensive toward them. And above all, don't refer to them as a piece of crap. You got it?

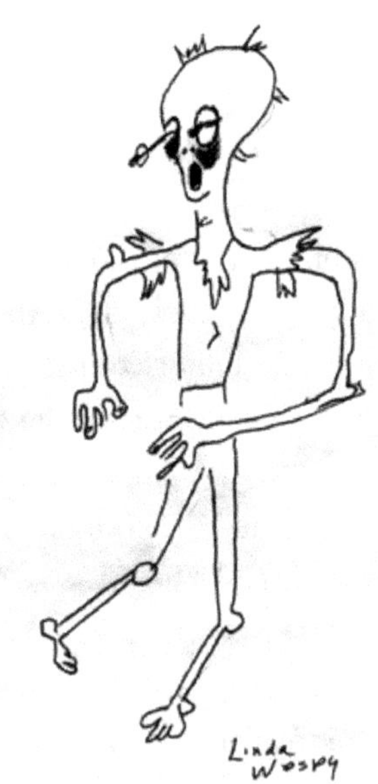

The Catch so Deadly

"Off we go me mates after the boat's loaded up, the pods are loaded and secured, and the bait is on. Then we are ready to shove off. I heard there's a storm brewing, so it's not going to be easy for us out there. It looks like we'll have a battle on our hands." And it was a battle on the sixth hour at sea.

The tempest was ready for them with its battle axes fixed, its black clouds shaped like the devil's head, its leaning out over the horizon with its cheeks full of air to blow and blow. The wind was coming from the north, the south, the east, the west with no rhythm to know where to steer the boat. Rogue waves were rolling over the side. Then the captain had to count the men to see if any were swept out at sea and gone down to Davy Jones's Locker.

The tempest was gaining more strength to make it worse for the men with plenty of air left in its cheeks. The deck hands were still tossing the pods over the side and bringing them back up while trying not to get killed by all the shifting heavy machinery and swinging pods on the deck. Sometimes the pods were empty and other times full. When they were full, the risk wasn't so bad, but the empty ones made them wish they would have stayed home. Life's not so easy out there on the stormy seas, but in order to feed his family, one has to do what he has to do. Such is the life of a crabber on the Bering Sea.

Love's Religion

Love's religion is of the highest order with no labels attached; no isms, no envy, and no intelligence that interferes with that deep feeling rooted from a love of all things, a cleaving to the Holy Spirit within us and a voluntary devotion to keep it flowing. Man made religion is an invention of disciplines, a reprimand for bad behavior and a guideline to stay on the path to its own apotheosis with a fear of straying from it.

Love in the highest order has no fear. It is the consecration of all religions. It is a mingling with the power of the Holy Spirit, the inner feeling in us all that takes us to that apotheosis with no fear of straying from it. It is an exhilarating ride. Since it is so deeply rooted in us, it makes us feel wholesome and joyful, devoid of any man-made religion that recruits us to become members of it and follow their own guidelines to reach their man-made apotheosis of love which we already have within us.

It makes us soldiers of its faith, enemies of other religions' faith, a hatred within us that keeps us from attaining a whole-hearted love. Hail to the man with no religion; with just a true feeling of love within him.

Back Scratching Celebrities

The other day while scratching my back, I came up with a brilliant observation. Since Michael Strahan scratches his back, he does the same thing I do. We must be of the same mold; brothers with itchy backs. The only difference is that I know him and he doesn't know me.

Since we both do the same thing though, we are equal in our endeavors. When our backs itch, we scratch them. Together we form a bond. He doesn't know it, but I do. Maybe you could call it a half bond; one who knows it and the other who doesn't.

Does that mean that I'm also famous, or half famous, or not at all famous, or half way to becoming famous since we are together a half bond? Maybe so.

I'm available to sign autographs at any time. The only difference is that Michael can sign a whole autograph while I can only sign half of one. It sure is a wonderful feeling these days, being half famous.

The Extremist

Extremism is in the disruption of peace and normalcy that is a common good that is established between nations. Ideology of each one is examined and accepted. Some ideals are moderated for the good of civilization. Each one is established with the good in mind and accepted in the hearts of the countrymen. Like a universal family each one abides by it and depends on a good familial relationship to survive.

Extremism comes out of the restlessness in the soul of man, too restless to live in peace and moderation and too restless to live with himself. Utopia is the ideal society with the ideals in the mind of mankind to live up to. It is too middle of the road for him; too moderate. Since his disposition is extreme in nature, too violent and restless, he cannot feel at ease in a peaceful surrounding. It is not the rules of moderation but his temperament that makes him break the rules. Extremism is a spark that grows into a flame that burns up all reason and leads to its own destruction.

Interior Anticipation

He is the best in the business; one helluva player. Besides being blessed with the strength of a gorilla and the agility and swiftness of a cheetah, he can see the play develop before the ball is snapped. With his prophetic visions, he can see every movement that is about to take place.

He can see the eyes of the quarterback dictating what was about to happen. He can see the right guard pulling to block for a run around the left side. He can see the slot receiver getting ready to get the handoff after a fake to the running back. He can see the right side of the defensive line expecting a run and moving over to the wrong side. He can see the containment man on the right side being sucked in to break his containment. He can see the safety moving up close to the line of scrimmage expecting a handoff to the running back. He can see the corner back and strong safety undecided whom to cover. Then he could see the ball carrier running sixty yards for a touchdown.

With his interior anticipation, he can do his best to make sure all what was about to happen doesn't happen. He is a valuable asset to any team. That is why he is the best in the business.

Aggression Management

Aggression is a paradox of good and evil with each seeking dominance in the soul of man. The good builds up society and the evil tears it down. It is the eternal energetic force in the will of mankind that yearns to be released through his deeds. There is no escape from its influence. It is the controlling element that determines how he manages his aggression.

If every person in the world was under the influence of the good aggression, there would be no more wars. In other words, there will always be wars, and there will always be the good that rebuilds civilization and tries to keep it safe, intact, and livable. Ever since Cain murdered his brother Abel there will be wars. If there was no aggression in the will of man, he would be a vegetable with no energy, drive, or desire to accomplish any task or endeavor.

Concience Authority

Thank God for the conscience within us; his innate moral law that's branded into our being at birth. Its presence is always there, but sometimes its influence is not. We can feel it when we do a good deed through our charity. We have a good feeling in our hearts and a more healthy, moralistic evaluation of ourselves from acting under its authority. It is our God given reward for following its orders.

We were created to be civil on this Earth. If we follow our conscience mandates, our Planet Earth will last forever. We can do our part by letting our conscience control us and letting its influence guide us. Through our charitable acts we feel better about ourselves and those who benefited from our charity.

When we can't feel or don't want to feel our conscience inside, it has no authority within us. The happier we feel depends upon its influence. It is always there even if we disregard it. By disregarding it, we have to substitute something else to make us happy; material gains or power? Power always belittles someone affected by it. Material gains are only objects that we cling onto for our temporary satisfaction.

Everybody wants to feel happy and satisfied. It is our moral obligation to let our conscience influence us. Since we were created to be civil, why not be civil?

Prospectors

Prospectors of yesteryear scaled the craggy cliffs with their mules, sifting pans, picks, blankets, rifles, food, whiskey, and enough supplies to last as long as it took to find the gold. They battled the elements; the weather, snakes, wild animals, and everything else that obstructed their quest.

Some prospectors are poets equipped with pen, an empty parchment, and a clear mind to find the mother lode. They find the soothing music and listen for the peace that flows through it so they can write about it. Its simplicity soothes the nerves and opens up the corridors to the heart. Its slow-moving melodies pull back the swift-moving words that clog the mind and massages them with the oils of the ambrosia fields.

The sweet, lazy ambiance of the music lies upon the jagged edges of anxiety that festers in the busy mind as it soothes them with its silky fingers. It teaches patience to the poets with their swirling words that long to be released to fill up the paper. Perseverance lies in the easy-going mood of the prose. It sits still and waits for the words to come to the surface to be written down, glorified, and refined.

Now that the busyness of the mind has been subdued by the pulse of the slow-moving music, it gave the words time to rise and open up the path to the mother lode so he can find the words that lay deep inside the jagged cliffs. At last the poem can be written.

Higher Learning

We owe all the knowledge we got from the man who invented the wheel and all the tribesmen he inherited "his" knowledge from. From this, the mechanics of transportion took root and branched out and became more sophisticated, and higher learning became the tool to understand it and make it viable. We as students of higher learning graduate ourselves as we understand each level of it and become a valuable asset to the needs of the corporations.

Our Final Days

Our waning days before the final day,
before God's divine plan for us
to die comes into effect,
are the days where we have control;
either days of great joy or days of misery
 while waiting to die while doing nothing
except staring at the walls
and feeling sorry for our lonely selves,

or greater days of eager anticipation.

 We enjoy doing something
to advance ourselves
through reading, exercising,
or learning a skill and working
toward perfecting it while
looking forward to the next day
when the knowledge of it
fills us full of an acquired satisfaction.

Knowledge and the pursuit
of knowledge is a joyful
 continual advancement
of the mind and soul until
our final day of expiration.

The time it takes to acquire it leaves
no time for us to feel sorry for ourselves.

9 788119 654833